T0128235

TWENTY BOSSES

Barney Hulett

authorHOUSE®

AuthorHouse™
1663 Liberty Drive
Bloomington, IN 47403
www.authorhouse.com
Phone: 1 (800) 839-8640

Published by AuthorHouse 08/03/2016

ISBN: 978-1-5049-6170-7 (sc)
ISBN: 978-1-5049-6148-6 (e)

Library of Congress Control Number: 2015918775

Print information available on the last page.

Vietnam 1968

"Home Sweet Home" in Vietnam, 1968

I WOULD LIKE TO DEDICATE THIS book, with much admiration, love, devotion and pride, to our granddaughters, Charity, Holly, Tiffani, Caroline, and Meagan. You are a source of much joy, to Nana and me. Our lives would not be complete without you. We wish you all the very best in your lives, and I feel deep down in my heart that each of you will achieve your goals. We do love each of you very much and may the world always be at your feet. Love you. Papa.

A special thank you to Kimberly Zuberbueler of Stonewall, Texas, who had the role of first reader and editor. Somehow, she was able to collect my memories and thoughts into something readable, and still maintain the style of my speech and thought process. This had to be a "Living Hell" for a teacher of English and Literature. "May God bless her forever."

FOREWORD

"WE HAVE FAITH, WE HAVE family, we have friends and we have had a lot of fun traveling down life's road. I have all this, plus I have an ace in the hole. I have Libby, and we will be together for all eternity."

One expects a book written by an employee of a famous person to be about their relationship with the famous. We expect the book to expose, exploit or salute.

Barney Hulett, pilot of presidents and prime ministers, has written an autobiography that is not about what you expect. But then again, Barney Hulett is full of unexpected surprises, so why shouldn't his book be?

I confess I felt a quiet groan coming on when I learned that Barney was writing a book. Barney had been my father's pilot during and after the Presidency, and, not seeing him as a writer, I was apprehensive.

My apprehensions proved totally unfounded. Not because Barney wrote a book deifying my father, but because Barney's book is not focused on deifying or vilifying Daddy. It's focused on telling an American love story. A farm boy falls in love with flying, "true love," and country. He survives multiple tours of war-zone duty and three Presidential administrations to live "happily ever after." All of this is peppered with a hysterical sense of humor, a heart of a romantic, and a real page-turning capacity to keep the reader engaged.

If you are looking for "kiss and tell," this isn't the book for you. But if you have the appetite for a well-written, poignant, and funny story about a man who lived the American dream, treasuring his "faith, family and friends and has had a lot of fun traveling down life's road," then you're in for a treat!

P.S. And for those who could use a little romance in their lives, what girl wouldn't die to have her husband say he has an "ace in the hole" because he will be with his wife into all eternity?!

Respectfully,

Luci Baines Johnson
Austin, Texas

TWENTY BOSSES

1

WHAT IN THE WORLD WAS this old country boy doing in this situation? Here I was three thousand feet above the jungles of Laos with one engine shut down and the other engine beyond the heat limitation because of the additional load to maintain altitude to safely clear the mountains. If that was not enough gray hair material, the closest safe landing strip was one hundred miles to the east in Vietnam.

* * *

I was born in the Panhandle of Nebraska, sand hill country, where the temperatures are as extreme as anywhere I have been. Folks have to be as tough as an old boot to want to live there. I guess I did not measure up to that standard because I left there as soon as I was old enough to be on my own. Having come into this world in the year 1928, I was too young to serve my country in World War II.

I would have to say that the one event that influenced my life was that an Air Force base was constructed next to our farm. When it was nearly completed, the 507th Parachute Infantry Regiment arrived for training. The sky was filled with C46 and C47 cargo aircraft towing G4A gliders. Anywhere we would look, we would see soldiers floating down to the earth on their parachutes, and the gliders, filled to capacity with men and equipment, would release from their tow plane and float down to their designated landing area.

On one occasion, one of the gliders missed his landing area and came to earth in a pasture next to our house. What a thrill it was to actually see one of those birds from the sky up close! More joy was to come shortly as a Jeep and a trailer arrived, and poles were set up with a wire across the top. A towrope was attached to the glider and then looped across the wire. A short time later, a cargo plane arrived, which flew directly between the two poles and only a few feet above the wire. A hook extended from the aircraft caught the loop and jerked the glider airborne. The engines on the cargo plane labored and smoke came from them, but they were airborne.

At that very moment I knew that was for me. I had to be part of this. I had to fly and do what I could for my country. It was a helpless feeling not being of age, where I could accomplish my ambition immediately. As the days passed, I formulated what I would do. I would save my money and take flying lessons. The airport at the time was near my hometown. It was really what you would call a "cow pasture" airport. An old hangar-type building was the only structure. Maintenance on the small aircraft was performed in this building. Two sod runways, favoring the prevailing winds, were present in this cow pasture. Outlined with old automobile tires, these runways were mowed during the summer months, and the snow was plowed in the wintertime. This is where my new life really began.

A short time before my sixteenth birthday, I checked in at the airport and was assigned an instructor pilot. I was amazed because my instructor pilot was a lady. Louisa Benna was petite and very pretty. She was home for a while between flights of ferrying bombers to Africa. Being so short in stature, I often wondered how she could reach the rudder pedals on those big bombers.

That first flight was something I will never forget. We bounced down the sod runway in a 65 horsepower Porterfield airplane. All at once, roughness became silky smooth, and we were in the air. Even now, some twenty thousand hours of air time later, I can still remember that deep feeling of slipping away from earth. This was it! I was sure that this was for me. I was in my element. I completed my first supervised solo flight on my sixteenth birthday. It was mandatory at that time to have had a total of eight hours of dual instruction before the student could fly the aircraft solo. That was exactly as much as I had the first time I flew the aircraft by myself.

As that time arrived, my instructor got out of the Porterfield, put a sand bag in the seat she had vacated, and told me in no uncertain terms that she would be watching every move the sand bag and I made. I aligned the aircraft with the old automobile tires and applied power. A lifetime later, I was airborne and in control of the aircraft. If adrenaline could be measured by some method, I am sure that mine was at the top and running over.

In the back of my mind, I could hear my instructor, "Do not climb too steeply; watch your instruments." In this case, there were only about four of them to scan. "Keep your wings level; make sure that you have the correct altitude when you make your turn to the crosswind leg. Be alert; rotate your eye scan from the cockpit to outside the aircraft and then back. Make a standard turn to downwind at the correct altitude, and then get your pre-landing check started."

The carburetor heat was pulled to the "on" position, and then just opposite my touchdown point, I pulled back the throttle to the idle position and then started my descending turn to the base leg. I watched the airspeed and kept descending. In the back of my mind, I could hear my instructor telling me, "Do not slow up too much on your turn to final approach." If you are too slow in the turn, a stall will occur and a spin could follow with not enough altitude to effect a recovery.

Then I was on final approach with the aircraft aligned with the runway. This was it. I descended down to the runway and just a few feet above the grass surface, I held the aircraft off the ground by bringing the stick back and effecting the stall at the exact moment that the landing gear touched down on the runway.

I had done it! On the landing roll-out, my instructor, who had positioned herself next to the runway, gave me a thumbs-up and then motioned me to do it again. I went two more times around, and then taxied to the hangar, which was followed by the traditional shirt-tail cutting. My nickname was inscribed on the piece of cloth with the date and then tacked on the office wall. I had soared with the eagles and returned safely. My life would never be the same again.

Louise Benna, wherever you might be, I hope you are in good health and enjoying happiness. If by an act of fate, you are reading this, I want you to know that when you said that you would take the stick out and beat my head with it if I bounced one more landing, I believed every word you said.

Shortly after my first solo flight, I violated FAA regulations, and this is the only time I ever did. Well, at least it is the only one I will admit to. I went to the airport, rented an airplane, flew over, and landed in the pasture next to our farmhouse. I talked my dad into going up with me. He thoroughly enjoyed his first flight. At that time, all I could think of was flying. Consequently, my school studies and work habits suffered. Every time I got some money in my pockets, I would head for the airport. About half of the flying time was with an instructor pilot and the other half was solo flight, practicing what we had covered before.

I had almost enough flying time to take my check ride for my private license when I became old enough to legally enlist in the service of my country. I enlisted in the Army. I then went to Fort McClellan, Alabama, to complete three months of Infantry basic training. It was hot and dusty with long days and short nights. Our days consisted of: calisthenics, bayonet training, firing of weapons, care and cleaning of equipment, map reading, tactics, bivouac involving field exercises, obstacle course, and more that has been forgotten. One I will never forget was KP duty, where I learned how to clean the pots and pans.

Anniston, Alabama, was the town next to the fort, and as I remember and was to find out later, it was typical of most towns next to military bases. Anniston had bars, pawnshops, second-hand car lots, and the always-present ladies, who helped the military police patrol the streets and bars. I do remember that there was a very nice U.S.O. where a soldier could go and relax if one was fortunate enough to get some time off.

During the last month of basic training, I received verification that I would be going to parachute school after my completion of basic training. This was great. It was what I had requested when I enlisted. I eagerly looked forward to the day that I would complete my training. A prayer to God to not ever let me come back to this place was evidently answered because during all of my military career, I did not have to return.

During that time, troops were normally transported by trains. After completion of our training, those of us who were selected for parachute school were taken by trucks to the railhead and loaded on a troop train bound for Fort Benning, Georgia.

On our arrival at Fort Benning, we off-loaded into a new world. Lined up by the platoons we were to fill, there stood our new "bosses." I could not believe my eyes. There they stood with their backs as straight as ramrods; the creases in their uniforms looked razor sharp; the parachute emblem was embroidered on their caps; silver wings were pinned on their chests, and their pants legs bloused into spit-shined jump boots. They had to be Supermen, and there we stood with duffel bags over our shoulders, having slept in our uniforms on the train. We looked like something the old cat, who did not know what he was doing, had dragged home.

I had no further time for observation as our training began immediately. The command came, "Assume the position. Give me ten. Give me twenty. Give me fifty." Push-ups, push-ups, push-ups. While performing this task, we had to count each one with the loudest voice we could muster.

The routine that started the next morning did not vary during the rest of the training. Reveille sounded at 0400 hours, and ten minutes later we were in company formation. A right face, double-time command would be given, and we were off on our morning run. We ran one time around Larson Air Field, which I calculated to be almost four miles. Next came breakfast, followed by a short break to clean the barracks and ourselves. Then we would fall-out again to be marched to the parade field for calisthenics, better known as the dirty dozen. We started with only one or two repetitions, but by the time our jump training was completed, we were in high numbers. The eminency of the course was physical fitness. Our classroom was the outdoors. Our class was usually conducted at the station we were to perform on. This included the forty-foot tower, the 250-foot high tower, parachute landing-fall platform, and the parachute rigging area.

We next had demonstrations by our instructors, which was followed by us trying to do the exercises. Harassment of a physical form was used to install a fast and obedient reaction to any command. Push-ups were given for any alleged infraction. Our numbers dwindled away. As it was a voluntary course, all a soldier had to say was that he had enough. He would pack his duffel bag and by nightfall, he would be gone. We lost other men along the way. Some did well on the physical portion but could not jump out of the towers. Others, on their first jump from an airplane, came back down with the airplane. As I recall, only about one-third of us, who started the training, had the pleasure of pinning the silver jump wings to our uniform.

With training complete, we had about a week of light duty while orders were being cut, assigning us to our new duty stations. We strutted around the training area, intimidating those who were still in the hell we had just come from.

Of course, we spent a night in sin city. Phoenix City, Alabama, was just across the Chattahoochee River and at that time was wide open. You name it, and they had it. The peanut farmers who frequented the bars were probably as tough as we thought we were, but some things have to be proven. Fist fights would extend from the bars to the bridge, and on the Georgia side, taxi cabs would be waiting to take us back to the fort. I am not sure, but I believe some from both sides of the conflict were thrown off the bridge into the river.

Forty years later, I flew some people to Georgia and had the occasion to spend the night in Columbus. I rented a car and drove out to Fort Benning. It was like being back in the past. The jump towers were still the same; the sawdust pits, where I sweated part of my life away, were still the same; the temporary building, where we lived, was still the same, and I have to admit that it was beautiful.

The transfers were published and put on the company bulletin board. I was ordered to report to the 82nd Airborne Division in Fort Bragg, North Carolina. When I reported to the replacement company, I was assigned to the 504th Parachute Regiment. It was very exciting for me to be a part of this elite unit. The division had a tremendous combat record and was completely staffed with above-average personnel. The unit, which had returned from Europe, had lost key personnel in combat and had had discharges from the service after returning, but the cadre was intact and set about returning the unit to its former proficiency. It was exciting with a lot of hard work, but it was fun.

We still made our early morning runs, but now they were battalion and regimental size. I had noticed that on really cold days (and it can get cold in North Carolina), the officers would be there when the units were formed up for the run, but they did not run with us. One exceptionally cold morning, we had stripped down to T-shirts and were prepared to start our run, when a Jeep drove up and General Gavin hopped out. "Slim Jim," as his men affectionately called him, began stripping down to his T-shirt. It was a chain reaction. I do not know how the word was passed, but I do know that a record was set by our officers in removing their overcoats and jackets. We all made the run on this day.

Small unit training began shortly after my arrival. We still started the day with the morning run, and I felt blessed with the fact that I could run. Once I got my second wind, I felt like I could run all day long. I actually looked forward to the runs.

The training started with the squads and platoons, and then we went into company size. I believe that at that time we were up to strength in manpower. We had company size drops, carrying full equipment, and after parachuting in, we would carry out our mission. Periodically, we would return to the firing ranges to fire the weapons assigned to each soldier. Gradually, the company training was blended into battalion and regiment. Then training on a division level was performed. The grand finale was a maneuver of division size. I truly believe, that upon completion of this, we were combat-ready.

Back at the fort, after our return, duties lightened up somewhat, and fun was had by all. Physical standards were upheld by playing different sports. Everyone participated; no benchwarmers were allowed.

About this time, I decided it would be nice if I had some transportation so I could whip around when I had some time off. If I could not fly in the air, I would fly down the roadways. A motorcycle is what I needed. The very next weekend, that I did not have to pull any duty, I headed for the town just outside the fort and began my search for wheels.

There were plenty of motorcycles to pick from. I found one that I liked and let a smooth-talking salesman help talk me into buying it. I was slightly embarrassed when the man asked me if I wanted to try it out. I had never ridden a bike before. "No," I said to him. "I like it and will take it now."

If that salesperson is still living, he is probably still laughing when he thinks about my departure from his lot. It had to look like a one-man Keystone Kops episode. By the time I arrived at the main gate of the fort, I had everything under control except the starting and stopping. I was lucky because the MP waved me on. I did learn to ride it and had lots of enjoyment from it.

I discovered one thing from my motorcycle venture. When you are in the learning stage, you are less likely to have an accident. Only when you think you have mastered it, you are more likely to take a few more chances than before and wipe-out time draws near.

I have done some dumb things in my life, really dumb, but the one I did with my motorcycle should make me king of stupidity. I had ridden over to western North Carolina and was returning after nightfall. It was cold, and I had not dressed properly. I fell in behind a semi-trailer truck and discovered that by staying only inches from the trailer, I was out of the wind and the cold was tolerable. I get goose bumps just writing about it. All that trucker had to do was to tap his trailer brakes, and I would have been squashed like the bug that hits your windscreen. I stayed in that configuration all the way down the mountains and for fifty miles more. As I think back, the driver must have known that I was behind him and did not want my death on his conscience.

The end of my enlistment was getting close and a decision had to be made——go, or stay. A baby sister had been born during my absence, and being of a young age, I still possessed strong family ties. I took my discharge and went home. I could not observe any major changes in the town and surrounding area.

I immediately applied for flight training under the G.I. Bill of Rights and shortly was back in the air again. The training was conducted at the air base, which had been abandoned by the military after the war was over. We could land and take off numerous times before we would use up the length of the 9,000-foot runway.

My hometown was primarily a railroad town. It had a repair area where the boxcars were repaired, a roundhouse where the locomotives were serviced, and a large train yard where trains were made up and sent on their way. Outside of the farmers and ranchers who lived in the area, the railroad was the backbone of the town's economy. Nearly every family had some kin working for the railroad. As a matter of fact, my dad worked there most of his life and retired from the railroad. So it would only be natural that I would make out an application for employment with the railroad.

I was hired as a fireman on steam engines. The first engine that I fired on was a hand-fed switch engine that was used to put trains together in the train yard. The fireman had to shovel the coal into the firebox. A nice, even fire in the firebox was demanded at all times. Clinkers would form to destroy the nice, even fire, and you would have to use a long metal rake to push them out of the way. There was no time to rest. The firebox had an endless appetite for coal, and the hard-nosed engineer was always yelling for more steam.

After my apprenticeship on the train yard donkey was completed, I graduated to an engine on the road. It was of the large class steam engine, and it had stokers, which conveyed the coal to the firebox. The fireman still had to control the amount of coal needed for maintaining the required fire. Also, the water level had to be just right. Plus, those damn clinkers had to be moved aside! A day's work on a local freight train consisted of picking up or setting out freight cars anytime there was more than one track. A through-freight train would only stop and go into a siding to let another train pass. We did not pick up or set out cars. At the end of the line, we would stop, eat, and check into the bunkhouse to sleep. Eight hours or more later, we would bring another train back to our home base. It did not take me long to figure out that some members of our crew had a wife on both ends of the line.

Then I got the opportunity to work in the diesel electric engine. It was great. My clothes did not get dirty, and the work was not hard. Every so often I would go back through the units checking water levels and checking for fuel injectors that might be stuck. If any irregularity was found, about the only thing I could do was to take that particular unit off the line. Other than checking my units periodically, I would plant myself in a nice big chair and watch the world go by. Until I had enough seniority, I worked off the extra board. I was on call if they needed me, but days might go by between calls. When the call did come, it might be on a passenger train or on a local freight.

I had my first exposure to the union on a local freight run. We had left the home terminal at night, setting out and picking up cars. Delays, caused by setting on the sidetracks allowing other trains to utilize the main line, had extended our time frame greatly. As we were pulling into our destination, I noticed that the engineer was checking his watch. At a precise time, he set the air and stopped the train. As he grabbed his metal suitcase, he said, "Time's up." With more than half our train still on the main line, we walked into the train yard. A crew had to be called to bring our train the last mile. They received four hours' pay for this duty. Remember this when you think an item should not be so expensive.

Seniority was "God Almighty" in the railroad systems at that time. It was not who was the best qualified, but who had been on the job the longest. Therefore, the old heads were running the fastest passenger trains, transporting hundreds of people. I think at that time in the engine service employees could work until seventy years of age. Most performed very well, but a few of them were becoming close to dotage.

One old engineer in particular would ask me my name, and when I told him, he would reply, "Oh, yes, a new man." This would happen even though I had made the last six runs with him. I thought maybe he was pulling my leg until I checked with other firemen and was told that he just could not remember things. He must have suffered a melt-down in that portion of his brain. I had to set the air and stop the train more than once because the old engineer was nodding, and we were getting into trouble.

I believe there is a time when age overcomes experience. Reaction time is slower; the brain may not function as quickly, and actions which had been performed almost automatically, now had to be thought about beforehand. Since then, the mandatory retirement age has been lowered.

During slack time when the number of trains that were running was cut back, the train crews were also cut back. Some engineers were sent back to fireman duties, and we, on the extra board, were out of jobs.

Shortly after that, I discovered that I could go to work as a switchman in the train yard. I was part of a crew that worked with the switch engine crew to put together the trains. It entailed taking trains apart that had arrived and sorting out cars for different destinations and putting them into the proper trains.

It was outdoor work, and in the wintertime it was tough. The boxcars would be covered with snow and ice. We would have to hang on the side of the boxcars so we could signal the engineer and direct him where to go. In daylight hours, arm signals were used, but at night we had to have a light in our hand. The hand brake control for each car was located at the top of the car, and many a time, I had to grab for something to hang on to when my feet would slip out from under me. It was not much fun working in the snow and ice, compounded by darkness, with the boxcars slamming into each other. I had to stay alert. One of my co-workers was killed, when for some reason, he stepped between two cars as they were pushed together.

The new people usually were assigned the midnight to eight o'clock shift, and this presented the worst working conditions.

After our shift was completed, we would head for our favorite saloon. We would drink beer that was mixed with tomato juice, shoot pool, and relax for a few hours. Then it was off to bed for our required rest before starting the cycle again. It was a job—but I felt that something was missing.

I looked at the old heads who were married and had started families. They were saving a little money each payday, bouncing the Missus periodically, looking forward to a vacation in the Black Hills, and when that was over, back to the same old grind. Please do not get me wrong. This is the American way of life, the backbone of our greatness. God-fearing families, who work hard to educate their children and then help them to get started in a profession where they have a better life than their parents. But I had been exposed to a different life in the service and, frankly was a little homesick for it. A decision was made, and I headed for Denver and the recruiting office.

2

I WAS BACK IN THE ARMY again, and I will have to admit it really did feel good. I was assigned to the 11th Airborne Division at Fort Campbell, Kentucky. After a week or two of my re-enlistment, I arrived at Fort Campbell. The unit had just returned from Japan and still was in the process of settling in. I was put into a division headquarters company as a vehicle driver. There I met a man, who turned out to be the best friend I ever had. He had served in the 82nd Airborne Division during World War II as a combat medic. He had gotten out and started a family, and he and his wife now had a three-year-old girl. Somewhat like me, I think he missed the regimentation and the ordinance of military life. After he had been discharged following the war, he went to a little town in Texas to help his dad operate a service station. And after a few years of what had to be dull to a person who had been through so much during the war, he had re-enlisted in the Army.

As you will see later, I wonder how my life would have ended if I had not met this man and his family. They had a mobile home that was parked just outside of the camp, and I was a frequent guest for good home cooking.

While we were still both assigned to the same unit, we went on field exercises. At nightfall, whichever one of us pulled into the bivouac area first, would put up our two-man tent and have everything set up. This was especially nice because it always seemed to start raining as the last vehicle entered the area.

After the exercise was completed, we were assigned to regular units. I was sent to the 127th Combat Engineer Battalion, where if I remember correctly, our motto was, "We build or blow it up," and this was done under combat conditions. Even though we could serve as infantry, we were to be specialists in certain fields. This included a Bridge Unit, which could put a bridge across a river under enemy fire. At that time we did not have the capability of dropping large items, like bridge sections, so while the rest of the unit would parachute in, the bridge unit would come by trucks.

It was about the same time frame that I received notification that I would be going to demolition school in Virginia as soon as a quota was assigned to the division. When my friend asked me what my plans for the weekend were, I told him I did not have any. He said, "Why not ride down to Nashville with us? My wife's sister is coming to visit us, and you might want to meet her."

I have not made a lot of good decisions in my life, but I made the very best one when I said that I would love to go. When the airliner she was scheduled on arrived and taxied in to the ramp, I had a good vantage point sitting on a fence next to the exit gate. I had been shown some pictures of her, so I knew whom to look for. The ramp was pushed against the aircraft, and the passenger door was opened to off-load the arriving passengers.

Finally, she stepped into the doorway and for my very first time, I observed a very eloquent young lady. She was so pretty. She was wearing a large picture hat, a fancy dress, and high-heeled shoes, and she carried a small overnight case in one hand. The wind was blowing fairly strong, so as she descended the ramp, she had to decide whether to hold her hat or her dress down. She decided to save her hat. I truly believe that is the exact time I fell in love with Libby, and fifty-three years later, I am still in love with her. I truly believe that she was meant for me. The wind helped to disclose her long, pretty legs and thin, trim ankles, which are a sure sign of a thoroughbred.

She told me later that her first impression of me was not too good because I was just sitting there on the fence laughing at her, and I did not offer to help her carry her luggage. I truly do believe that I was not laughing, but I might have had a grin on my face. Her name was Elizabeth, but everyone called her Libby or Lib.

The next few days went by so quickly. My friend and his family took us to so many places. We went to Mammoth Cave and visited some of the Civil War locations, and I found out that Libby and I had a lot in common. She had been born and raised on a farm, and we were born in the same month and year, with me being eighteen days the senior. But we were not of the same astrological sign——and just maybe, this fact was conducive to our love for each other lasting for the last fifty-three years.

Libby was on her vacation from the telephone company in Fort Worth, Texas, and the time appeared to be going very quickly. We went swimming, sight-seeing, and I believe that I even rented a small airplane and took her for a ride. I did everything that I could think of to impress her. She was special, and I could not let her get away. Libby's parents came up to visit and take her back to Texas. They seemed really nice, but I could not tell what they thought of me hanging around. Good-bye time came, and it was tough, but we promised each other that we would write every day and call when we could.

It was only a week or so when we decided that we could not be apart, and we would be married. I could not get leave for a little while, but we set a date. The time finally arrived. My soon-to-be sister-in-law and soon-to-be niece and I drove to Dallas. We were married at the house of Libby's aunt and uncle. The house was beautiful and full of strangers. Not counting my bride, I knew only four people who were present. I met my best man, a friend of Libby's roommate, twenty minutes before the ceremony.

We had ten days before we had to be back to Fort Campbell. My friends told us to take their auto and use it on our honeymoon. Come to think of it, I wonder how my sister-in-law got back to Kentucky.

We spent our wedding night in Fort Worth. We then went on to spend a day or so with Libby's folks and then on to Nebraska for some time with my parents. When we got to Nebraska, Libby got a taste of what I had just been through. She did not know any of them, and I am sure she found them strange, but we had each other and that was all that mattered to us.

Years ago I got in the habit of telling people, when they would ask (and they always seem to do just that), "How in the world did you two people get together when one of you came from Texas and the other one from Nebraska?"

My reply was, "I was a paratrooper in the 11th Airborne Division at Fort Campbell, Kentucky, and when I met Libby, she was a Go-Go dancer in a beer joint in Clarksville, Tennessee."

Now, maybe my story telling has improved, or I have turned into a pathological liar, but people really believed me. The incident that really convinced me not to ever do this again was when one of my grandbabies said, "Was Nana really a Go-Go dancer?" I will not say any more about this except that she would have been a great one.

Back at Fort Campbell, with our honeymoon behind us, I found out that I was being sent to demolition school at Fort Belvoir, Virginia. We decided that while I was in school, Libby would stay with her sister and brother-in-law, and when I returned, we would find our first home.

I really did enjoy demolition school. I was so fascinated with the fact that I could make material and people disappear. The term "blow up" is always used, but whether it is up or down or in or out, it is still the same to me. The material is not present any longer. One phase of the course was booby traps, and it intrigued me ever so much. It was your brain against the enemy. So many devices were available, and the main principle, with many variations, was pressure. The application of, or the release of, pressure would cause bad things to happen. Any normal action, which you as an individual would automatically perform, would get you in deep trouble.

We would even booby-trap our classmates. Nothing was sacred, and we would always know when someone had fallen prey to our endeavors because an M-80 firecracker would be attached to the device. At that time there were only two means of causing explosives to detonate––electric or non-electric. It would be so much more fun now, with the sophisticated gear that is available. We practiced laying and recording mine fields, followed by breaching and removal of the same. The fun of this was the fact that the mines could be booby-trapped and during their removal would detonate.

Part of our class was responsible for the laying of the mines and another part would have to pick them up. We worked with all the different types of explosives and learned how to calculate the amount required for each job. Our final exam was to plan and carry out a demolition of a bridge. I later stole this idea and used it when I returned to my unit and helped to set up a division school. The theory of explosives is just that––a theory. The book would tell you what the explosives should do under certain conditions. Maybe they would and maybe they would not. I think that one factor was what made working with explosives so very interesting.

The "TV shot" of the skyscraper being dropped directly down on its foundation is a prime example of master craftsmen at their best. Each beam and each support has to be cut at just the exact time, and the amount of explosive used has to be absolutely correct. We were instructed in the use of shape charges, which were of a conical design. This design directed nearly all of the explosive force into a small area. This could be used to penetrate several inches of steel. I would like to have used one of these charges on a big, old safe, but with my luck, it would have burned up everything inside.

We also improvised a shape charge out of a Number 10 can and plastic explosive, but it was very difficult to get the angle of the cone just right. We were also schooled in the art of using the bangalore torpedo, which was used to blast through barbed wire or to detonate buried mines. It was a piece of metal tubing filled with high explosives and came in sections which were joined together so you could be a safe distance from the explosion. This blast-driven earth rod had just been developed, and we played with it. It was a long rod with a firing chamber at one end of it. We would pre-start it into the earth, insert a can of black powder into the firing chamber, and detonate it. The force of the explosion would drive the rod into the soil, and then with my trusty extraction bar, I could pull the rod out of the earth. Once removed, there remained a hole big enough to place several loops of primer cord.

Detonate the primer cord, and you had a hole big enough to lower a .40-pound cratering charge into. These charges were used to blow out bridge abutments. TNT was used the most in those days because of its safety feature. It did not shock very easily. As a matter of fact, you could fire a 30-caliber into it, and it would not detonate. Dynamite was fairly stable unless it had been subjected to an extreme temperature, either hot or cold. I did get into trouble with dynamite at a later date because of this characteristic. I really did enjoy this course at Fort Belvoir, and of course, it was directed by the top demolition personnel who were available to the military at that time.

Back to Fort Campbell, I was reunited with my love mate. She had gotten a small taste of what was to come in our military career. She was to raise our family, while I was somewhere else in the world, and believe me when I tell you, that to this day I still hear about it.

We found a place to live in Hopkinsville, Kentucky. A bedroom with kitchen privileges was suited to our budget. A fireplace that used coal heated the bedroom. It was at this time that I discovered that my wife had not seen coal before. Where she came from, they had always used wood for their heating. She would freeze during the day while I was on duty, even though the landlord would try to help her with the fire.

We did not have much money, but we had a lot of fun. My friend and sister-in-law would come over, and the four of us would play pinochle by the hour. Every now and then my friend and I would be forced to change the rules just a little bit so that we could ensure that we won the game. But one day the girls got their hands on the rule book of pinochle, and not only that, I think that they got together some signs. Needless to say, it took all the fun out of the game.

I had been selected for a full-time job to help set up a demolition school for the division. We put together a two-week course to be attended by personnel from all the major units in the division who would have a need for this training. After a cycle or two, we had it running fairly smoothly—— with one exception.

We had requisitioned the blast-driven earth rod that I had used at Fort Belvoir. On my first demonstration everything connected with it went sour. It required three cans of black powder to drive it completely into the earth, but the red face portion of this demonstration had only started. I turned to my trusty extraction bar to remove the earth rod, and what should have been a task for one man, turned into six men on the extraction bar with no results. We dug it out with shovels, boxed it back up, and sent it back to Fort Belvoir with our recommendations. When they designed this rod, they had not considered the differences in soils. We had sticky red clay at Fort Campbell, in comparison to a sandy loam at Fort Belvoir. I never saw the blast-driven earth rod again.

About this time, we had some new procedures put into effect regarding payday activities. Normally, on payday we would report to the pay officer, salute, receive our pay, and if we did not have a required duty, the day was treated somewhat like a Sunday. We were off to do as we pleased, but now this all changed. In fact, we almost disliked seeing payday roll around.

Payday started with the entire division on the parade field displaying a full field layout followed by an inspection of the same. Then we had pack-up time and a "pass-in-review" by the entire division. By the time this was completed, and we marched back to the unit area, it was time for the noon meal, but even then payday activities were not complete. Those who needed medical shots had to report to the local dispensary and up-date their medical records. When we finally received our pay, the day was gone. Also, once a month, a twenty-mile march with full field pack had to be completed, with the last five miles being a forced march. This was nearly a double-time exercise. You really had to be in good physical condition, or you could not complete it.

Our Commanding General had a mania about trash lying along the roadside, so at designated times all units would be at their assigned area conducting a police call. Fifty feet above us in his helicopter would be the General making sure we had not missed any item, which did not grow there. On one of these occasions, as we could hear the helicopter approaching us, one of the men lay down on his back and, at full attention rendered the hand salute. The General must have noticed since his helicopter immediately landed, and the pilot obtained the man's name. That very day he was transferred to a "leg" or non-jump unit.

We had been at Fort Campbell about one year when our son was born, and we were so happy. Prior to this event, we purchased our first mobile home. It was not much, but it was our home. It did not contain a bathroom, so we had to plan everything just right to prevent making the 100-yard trip to the communal bathhouse in the middle of the night.

A severe cold spell hit us, and even though Libby and I slept curled up like a couple of rattlesnakes, we were freezing. We added more blankets, and then we added still more—to no avail. We were so cold at night in bed. About springtime, we solved our problem. The cold was coming through the mattress from the bottom. We had been adding the blankets to the wrong side of us.

I was still instructing at our demolition school, and we were starting to get some positive feedback from the division units. We had been using dynamite on a ditching project when a really hot spell came along. I had been transporting and storing dynamite on a quarter ton trailer. When not using the dynamite, I would pull the dynamite trailer into the ammo dump and park it. I had been absent for a few days, and when I went by for an inspection of my dynamite, I discovered that I had a lot of leakage. Hot temperatures will allow the nitro to separate from the sawdust mixture that it is contained in. At this stage, it is very volatile in this unstable condition and any little bump could set it off.

When I reported this fact to my C.O., his comment was, "What are you going to do about it?"

I told him that my plan was to go out in the early morning when it had cooled down and gently pull the dynamite trailer to an area where there was not anything or anybody that could be harmed, and blow the dynamite and trailer in place.

He replied, "I will go with you because if anything happens to you, I will have paperwork from now on." So that is what we did, and by having my C.O. with me, he saved me from having to reimburse the government for the trailer.

In the school, we instructed our students that when they were crimping the time fuse to the blasting cap, they should insert the time fuse into the cap, place the crimping tool to the right location, and after raising their hands over their helmet, crimp the cap to the fuse. A student next to me did everything correctly except the pliers slipped down, and he cut the blasting cap completely through the very center where the bad stuff is. God was smiling down on us and let us get away with it.

3

THAT SUMMER I WAS INSTRUCTED to accompany a National Guard Infantry Division from Cleveland, Ohio, on the summer requirement to Camp McCoy, Wisconsin. I was to assist and advise on any demolition effort. It opened my eyes to a new world where everyone, regardless of rank, was called by their first name.

One day I slightly braced a sergeant when he called a colonel by his first name, and I was told, "No big deal. He works for me back in Cleveland." It was just a little bit hard for a paratrooper from the 11th Airborne Division to take, but I figured it out. Those units proved themselves in Vietnam and in Desert Storm.

At the conclusion of the exercise, there remained a large amount of explosives that had not been expended. The officer in charge informed me that they did not wish to haul it back to Cleveland, so we put all the remainder in one big pile and blew it up. This was really something to witness, somewhat like an atomic bomb being detonated.

Back at Fort Campbell and back in the demolition school, we had received permission to destroy all the condemned timber trestle bridges on the reservation. It was very interesting to plan and blow up these old bridges on the reservation. We worked it in with our demolition training and a lot of valuable training was obtained. We also learned that the streams were full of fish and with a very small amount of dynamite, we could catch all that was needed for a big fish fry.

Periodically, we would make practice jumps with full equipment and run a field exercise to update our training. Being a demolition man, I would jump with explosives. The blasting caps would be carried in a special felt-lined box, and the other explosives would be placed in an equipment bag that could be released about 100 feet from the ground. A web strap would still connect me to the bag, but the bag would be landing first and hopefully be out of the way when I hit the ground.

Now and then the quick releases would hang up, and then the bag and I hit the ground together. One jump was really made with ease. A strong wind was blowing, and it blew us away from the landing zone, putting us into the trees. I went into the position for a tree landing, and the canopy caught the top of the tree and gently let me down. When my descent was halted, I looked down and found my feet only inches from the ground. I hit the quick release and stepped out without a scratch, and my duty uniform was as clean as it was before the jump.

In the wintertime, we conducted an exercise in the northern part of New York State. It was really different jumping into the snow. Also, we were exposed to the use of snowshoes and snow skis. I did not do well with either of these.

A tank commander from a supporting unit came to me and told me that he had three tanks that had gotten into low areas and now were frozen in. He wanted us to set charges around them and blow them free. I told him that it would be very difficult to calculate the amount of explosive to use and that some damage might occur. He agreed that a little damage was better than leaving them there until spring. We got them loose with negligible damage, and the retriever pulled them out. This result exposed me to the good side of using explosives and was very gratifying.

Everything was going well on the home front. We were so happy with our baby boy. Libby had started out to breast-feed our son, but after a period of time, we found out he was not receiving enough to eat. The volume was fine, but the nutrition was lacking. Once he was put on real food, he was fine and slept the night through.

Libby learned to cook only after we were married. When she was growing up, her older sister had worked in the house with her mother, and Libby had helped her father on the farm. She could drive a tractor but did not have very much experience in the kitchen. She got a cookbook and started her experiments on me. After eating Army food for so long, my stomach could take almost anything, but now and then, I would suggest that she not try a particular dish again. She did not ever give up and turned out to be an excellent cook.

During this training period when Libby was learning to cook, I woke up in the middle of the night with a terrible stomachache. My first thought was, "My God, did we have something new to eat last night?"

I checked with Libby, and she was fine. I could not lie or sit down; the pain was almost unbearable. I walked around in the yard until daylight doubled up with pain, and then gave up and went to the base hospital. A short time later they had me in the operating room and removed my appendix just before it ruptured. I had a lot of fun giving Libby's cooking the credit for my predicament, but that was not true. I was really happy that my appendix had been removed because later on when I made a number of trips across the ocean on small ships, where a doctor was not present, I knew that was one less problem that I would have.

I attended the Division Jumpmaster School about this time. I had been leading the stick, or being the first man out, but really needed to be jumpmaster qualified. I also needed the jumpmaster qualification to receive my master jump wings. It consisted of five jumps, which were conducted with full equipment, and one or two of these were in the dark.

On the night jumps, instead of panels on the ground, we jumped on lights. The pilot or aircraft commander would give us a red or "get ready" light when he thought he was close to the drop zone, and a green or "go" light when he thought he was over the drop zone. It was up to the jumpmaster as to when he would jump his men. He would line up his foot, which was in the door, with the panel or light and then jump with his men following behind him. The panel or light would have been set up with an adjustment for the wind by the pathfinder unit, which had jumped into the drop zone prior to the main drop.

In the summertime, the reserve units from the Air Force would fly in from all over to jump us. They would have the old C-47 with only one jump door. We had been using C-82's and C-119's, which had two jump doors. We would still load the C-47's with as many jumpers as we could get in it. The catch was that only about half of the men could hook their static line to the static line cable before we got over the drop zone and the jump commenced. The other half would have to hook up as they moved toward the door. Picture a horseshoe and the right hand side of this would be trying to get their static lines hooked to a cable that was moving up and down about one foot because of openings that were taking place outside the aircraft.

There were several times when I went out of the door that I was not really sure that I was hooked up until I got the opening shock, which told me that my main chute was deploying. Of course, the riggers always told us that if the chute should happen to not open, just bring it back, and they would give us another one. My hat is off to the riggers. They were real professionals and would jump any chute that they had packed.

About this time, a new parachute was introduced, which appeared to be a big improvement over the one we were using. The T-7 parachute, which we had been using for so long, had a terrible opening shock, and if you had a bad body position when you left the door, you were almost certain to receive some riser bruises on your shoulder. The new parachute, the T-10, had a much less opening shock and was touted to be easier to steer.

In the name of research and development, they decided to get as many jumps on them as they possibly could in a short period of time. All master jumpers could, if it did not interfere with official duties, jump as many times as they wanted. It was a fun time. No equipment other than a steel helmet was used on these jumps. We would jump, hit the ground, roll up the chute, get on the truck, go back to the airfield, load on the aircraft, and jump again. We could do this until we were dog-tired.

Old timers, who did all of their jumping during World War II and shortly after, could tell you about the T-7 parachute. If the pilot did not get the aircraft slowed down to the right speed before the landing zone came up, the opening shock would make you think that you had been jerked right through your "you know what." The T-10 changed all that. Regardless of the added weight due to all the equipment you were required to jump with, the opening shock was not really that bad.

I do not know what the airborne units are using now, but I would bet they have even better chutes now than the T-10. During his college days, our son jumped with what he called a rag, while others were using what looked like a huge mattress over their head after deployment. Everything changes. I have no hard feelings about it. In fact, I feel really good about it because we did it the hard way.

The R.I.F. (or "reduction in force") came along about this time. Officers who had ten years or more of commissioned service were allowed to go back to their regular non-commissioned rank to complete their twenty years of service. Those who did not meet this criterion but had a good background could, if they so elected, revert back to enlisted status. Of course, some of them, who did not have very much time invested in the military, just said good-bye and went back to being civilians.

My friends and I would sometimes go out to the Rod and Gun Club to shoot trap and skeet and of course have a few beers. I happened to get acquainted with a sergeant who was in charge of the club. He had been a colonel, and the R.I.F. had sent him back to the enlisted ranks. Of course, the pay was not as good, but he was happy as a hog in a barrel of slop. He was having the time of his life running the club. He also told me about a recreation area which was being built on Kentucky Lake about eighty miles from the fort. Here is the nice part––he also mentioned that the division was looking for someone to run it. The engineers in my unit had cleared the area, and the division had moved in ten new mobile homes. I guessed I had enough connections in my unit and in the division to get the job.

We moved into one of the mobile homes and became the overseer of the area. We also had ten boats and motors that went with the mobile homes. Soldiers would sign up for these on a first-come, first-served basis. Libby, our one-year-old son, and I had a ball out there on the lake. We would get up early in the morning and get out on the water and fish. This had to be the proverbial bird nest on the ground. We would only go back to the fort to shop for staples, payday, or to make a pay jump. It was great. During the week, we were almost by ourselves, and we made the most of it. It was almost like we were not in the Army. This phase of our lives may have had some influence on what was to happen next. We had made several trips back to Texas, so the grandparents could see their grandson. On these trips, it was discussed that it would be nice to live there with Libby's parents close to us and their grandson. My enlistment was completed, but I was serving the remainder of an extension imposed by President Truman. When that period expired, we took the discharge and headed home to Texas.

We had our very own big house on a ridge about a mile from Libby's parents. I was farming with my father-in-law and using his equipment.

There was not any money until the crop was sold. Therefore, I was working part-time at a gas station and going to school two nights a week under the G.I. Bill. I would report to school at a designated time and play dominoes until it was time to go home. I never opened a book but I received a check each month. It wasn't much, but it helped to put food on the table.

Some in my dominoes class went on to bigger and better things. One became a district judge; several went into the less honorable field of politics; some stayed in the community and carried on the traditions of their forefathers. I think I was the only person in my class to make the military a career.

During this time, there were good times and bad times. A baby daughter was born, who was perfect in every way and was to bring us much joy.

We jokingly referred to our home as "poverty ridge," but in reality, that is what it was. A family of rock squirrels moved under the porch of our house, carrying fleas and possessing other undesirable traits. I was determined to remove these unwanted rodents from their illegal position. I had very little trouble shooting the first half of these fleet-footed little fur-balls, but the other half called on their survival instinct and made it tough for me. They would hear the screen door open, and under the porch they would go. Libby did not like it much, but my only alternative was to shoot through the screen door with a promise to replace it after the project was completed. It took a few days to get all of them, but soon I was the "King of the Ridge."

We were poor in the material sense, but we had fun. We were fairly active in our church, had our friends, most of whom had watched Libby grow up. Our son adored his grandfather and followed every step he made. It has been said that people with very little will accept that fact, live with it, and still enjoy life to its fullest. This may very well be true, but it was so very difficult for me to believe that this was what God had planned for my family and me.

It had been the year that had less rainfall than any of the old-timers could remember. I had killed a snake, and our chickens found it and ate it. This resulted in the chickens getting the limber neck and dying. Our hogs got the cholera, and we were burning dead pork every day. The crowning blow was the castor beans. It was a new crop where the beans were used in the process of making oil for jet planes. They did very well in an arid climate, which we certainly had that year. It was hot, hard work picking them, and on the way to the market place, a tailgate came loose, and I scattered them down the highway.

When I got home, Libby and I talked about our future. It would be so difficult to leave, but life looked so much like a dead-end road. We looked around at our neighbors and figured out that what they had was the very best that we could expect. If they had a good year, they were fine. If they had a so-so year, then the next year they had to borrow to put in their crop. Sure, they survived and raised God-fearing families who survived and went on to make a name for themselves in the world, but I had a really hard time acquiescing to put my loved ones in that position.

It was a very difficult decision to make, one that was not made easily or quickly. We were happy being a part of Libby's family and entering into the community and its activities. The people that we met in the church were our neighbors. Everyone we came in contact with would do anything to help us, and they were genuinely interested in us and what happened to us. They were just good country people who believed in a supreme being and in each other. It would have been such a beautiful life except for one thing––we could not make a decent living and do the things we planned for our children.

If we went back in the service, we would be leaving that family, but one fact we were sure of was that we would be going back to our military family, and it truly is a family. Military families are bonded together by the hardships, such as the long separations from their loved ones, being apart from parents and siblings, plus living in a foreign land with children. It had been easy enough to make that decision when it was just me––but now I had a family and responsibilities that would change the lives of others forever.

It was Christmas, a time to celebrate a birthday and to be with loved ones who believed as we did. We had a wonderful time with all of us together, and it started a procedure that has become a tradition with our family. We always make a special effort for all of us to be together on this great day, but after the holidays, we have to face reality and decide what we must do. We were happy and had a lot of fun on very little; in fact, we required very little in material things to survive. A big deal for us was to pop some popcorn and fix a jar of Kool-Aid and go to the drive-in movie once or twice a month, but now things had changed. We had two children to think of, not only now, but also with an eye on the future.

4

I MADE A TELEPHONE CALL TO my ex-commanding officer at Fort Campbell and asked him what rank I could retain if I came back into the service. He said he would check it out and get back with me, which he did the very next day. I would only lose one stripe because I had not yet been out a year. I gathered up my old uniforms, put them in our car, told my family good-bye, and also told them we would be together soon, and I headed east. It felt so good when I held up my right hand and swore to uphold and defend my country. I was home again, not to leave until death or retirement.

The paperwork was completed in a day or two, and I was assigned back to my old unit. It was "old home" week! There were a few new faces, but other than that it was nearly the same. One thing that did change was my new duties. I went to work in battalion operations with my primary duty being to schedule required training.

The second day on my new job found me at the airfield putting on a parachute. That had been one of the things I had thought about a lot when I was burning up in the peanut field. It would be so much fun stepping out into the clean, clear, cool air. Everything was going my way, with the exception of being separated from my family, and I was working to correct that. It was not too long until we were a family again.

We purchased another mobile home, and this time we were living high on the hog. It had two bedrooms, and wonder of all wonders, it had an indoor bathroom. It even had a bathtub. We had it moved back to the very same park where we had lived before. Some of our old neighbors were still there, and things were looking up. At least we knew there would be a payday, and we knew exactly how much we would receive. The ten months that we spent in Texas had really set us back in the monetary area.

As a matter of fact, it was several years before we reimbursed all the good people who had helped us.

I was kept busy in my new job. It involved a lot of paperwork, which I did not enjoy very much, and to this very day, I still do not like it. I guess one reason for the dislike was that I was not good at it. I loved the outdoors, and the idea of being at a desk all day really turned me off. Our units had to be spot-checked so that was my excuse for jumping in a Jeep and getting out in the field.

One day some paper came across my desk that was to change my life drastically. The Army had decided they would try a new concept of moving troops into battle zones other than dropping them in by parachute. They would, when possible, bring them in by helicopter. Up until now, the helicopter had been used exclusively for medical excavation and rescue. The helicopter program was going to be greatly enlarged, and they needed pilots. This was it, and what I really wanted to do! I would be flying!

I got busy with the paperwork, and I took the required physical. Then I sat back and waited for the painfully slow, but steady, paper process to complete its journey. It was three months before I received any word at all. When it did come, it was worth the wait. I was accepted and had a reporting date for my class.

It also recommended that no dependents accompany the student. Poor Libby. She had a decision to make. Should she stay at Fort Campbell, or return to Texas? She elected to go home, which was a practical choice, because we were pretty sure not to be reassigned to Fort Campbell.

Fort Rucker, Alabama, located just outside of Dothan, Alabama, was the home of the helicopter school and later was to become the aviation center. As a matter of fact, it may well have been Camp Rucker when I went there the first time.

I reported in and was briefed on what to expect while there. It was an accelerated course to include teaching us to fly helicopters and making officers out of us at the same time. We were to be in the classroom half of the time, and the other half was to be spent on flying activities. The upper classmen could not wait to tell us the good news. A psychiatrist would interview us before we started the course. This procedure had just been started by the Army. In fact, the class ahead of us had been the very first ones tested.

They had a horror story to tell us. About one-fourth of the class who had reported to school with them, had packed their bags and left after their interview with Doctor Farouk. Of course, with a name like that, he was to be called, not to his face but elsewhere, Dr. Fruit Cake.

This was serious. Dr. Fruit Cake had our careers in his hot little hands. I do not anger easily, but this really upset me. How could this S.O.B., in one interview, determine that you were unfit to fly? So when my turn came to be interviewed, I had made up my mind that I just did not like him. If by some chance, we could have met before, then I knew that I could hate him. No one person, other than the Almighty, should have the power to say who will stay and who will go!

His first question involved my sexual thoughts toward my mother, and I knew the route I had to take. I would lie, lie, lie, and hope to be forgiven later. I did not give a straight or completely truthful answer to any of his questions. I remember that I never once showed any irritation to his very sensitive and very personal questions. I was calm, cool, and collected. I just looked him dead in the eye and lied.

I just knew that I was gone almost before my bag was unpacked. When the list came out, about one-third of my class was gone, but I was still there. I had passed whatever test it was. Later on, I tried to analyze how it worked and what really happened. I knew Dr. Fruit Cake had tried to make me mad and upset so that I would lose my composure. Then I decided, what the hell, maybe a liar can fly helicopters.

After my retirement from the Army, I took all the courses I could on psychology, even child psychology, and I understood what Dr. Fruit Cake was doing. About the time we were finishing helicopter school, we received some feedback on Dr. Fruit Cake. He had let a few continue the course. Two of these people, whom he considered marginal, had accidents, and the others had washed out of the course along the way.

The ground rules were explained to us, and they were simple. Tactical officers and upper classmen were not to harass us during the classroom training or after we had reported to the flight line; however, the rest of our hours belonged to them, and they made the most of it.

We operated on the merit system. Boots not shined properly—— demerits; uniform not correct——demerits; billets not clean and left in disorder——demerits.

The only difference between flight school and jump school was that in jump school when the sun went down, you were even——but not here. The demerits piled up on you and dragged you down. The only way you could lighten the load was to work them off on free time, which meant the weekend.

We were assigned to a cubicle, and I cannot for the life of me remember my roommate's name, but I do remember that he reminded me of the character "Pigpen" in the *Charlie Brown* cartoon. I knew that I was not the neatest person in the world——but compared with my roommate, I was three-star.

It did not take me very long to realize that I would never get a weekend off. I was destined to spend weekends and free time in the company area. We had about a week of classroom, and then we reported to the flight line. It was super.

There were rows of training helicopters; I met my instructor, and I went on my orientation flight. Can you imagine this? I was sitting in a machine that rose up vertically two feet and then remained stationary in that position, then slowly moved down between the rows of helicopters. At the end of the rows, the nose of the machine slightly lowered and forward speed was gained swiftly.

This was great. I never thought it could be like this. This was really *flying*. I had so many options. I could move backwards and sideways. The flight was to be forty minutes in duration, but it seemed like five minutes. It was wonderful even though I did not have the controls.

The next day we left the flight line and went out to the country. We set down in a forty-acre field, and my instructor said, "It's yours. Pick it up and see if you can hover."

Hell's bells, this was going to be easy! I had watched my instructor's every move and knew exactly what to do. I got the R.P.M. up and slowly pulled up the collective pitch. It became airborne, and I was at a hover for one split second——and then I turned into Bozo the Clown. The forty-acre field was not nearly large enough. I was everywhere——up and down, sideways, and even going backward. It flashed through my mind, *How can he just sit there and let this happen to me?*

Finally, after what seemed to be an eternity, he said, "I have it," and he promptly brought it to a standstill in a hover. If there is something lower than humble, that was me. The next flight out, I did much better, and it was not very long until I felt that I was in control of the machine.

Anyone who is not helicopter qualified will not understand the feeling you have in a helicopter. Being fixed-wing rated, I had something to compare with, and there was not a comparison. You could do so many things with the chopper. I soloed in the prescribed time and went on my merry way. One flight would be with the instructor, and then I went solo to practice what he had demonstrated.

The classroom work was very good because we covered everything, even the maintenance of the machine. We also had classes in meteorology, map reading, tactics, and the use of the litter for evacuation of the wounded.

We were required to make one flight as a litter patient to give us some understanding as to how a wounded soldier might react in the litter. When it came to my turn, I was really not sure that this was something that I would enjoy. I was strapped in, lying on my back, and the lid of the litter was put in place. It was very much like being put in a coffin while you were still alive. Except for a small fiberglass area just above my face, I was completely enclosed. All that I could see, if I was brave enough to open my eyes, was the rotor head, the rotor blades, and of course, blue sky.

My thought was that at least the wounded would be hurting so badly that they would not care, and chances were that they would have been injected with morphine, anyway, which certainly would have helped me on that ride.

I had the same feeling of helplessness when I was required to ride in the cargo glider while in parachute school. It was at these times that I felt I had no control over my destiny and that made me feel very uncomfortable. At least in the cockpit or with a parachute strapped on, I was at ease knowing that if something did go wrong, I would have a fighting chance to ward it off. The helicopter saved so many more lives than it has taken, and even if some new machine should take its place, the helicopter should never be forgotten.

My roommate and I decided to go all out on our living quarters and pass the weekend inspection. We stayed up the entire night before inspection working our tails off by cleaning, dusting, and waxing the floor until it looked like a mirror. In fact, we would not even walk on it with shoes on. We put down towels and slid on them to keep from making marks on our shiny floor. Everything looked clean and proper. We were going to sail through this inspection with flying colors and be allowed to leave the company area and drink some beer and relax. We were ready. Let them come and see how sharp we were.

And they did come. Four upper classmen with white gloves on, and yes, you guessed it. Pigpen and I went down the tubes again. I was to discover later, when I became an upper classman, that it was so easy to find something out of place or unclean or incorrect that if you wanted to, *no one* could pass an inspection. Thank goodness, when Libby came to visit me, I was already an upper classman. Otherwise, we would have had to meet in the dayroom where the pool table was.

We had moved into the advanced stage of our helicopter training. Of course, we had practiced emergency procedures from the first day and not a day went by that we were not tested on them. The instructor pilot would roll off the throttle to simulate engine failure and an auto-rotation would follow to spot where you would hope you could land safely. Anti-torque failure would necessitate holding a lot of forward speed and running the helicopter onto the surface. We also would practice landing on a steep slope.

Then came the confined area. This *really* would put you to the test. It would be just a hole in the trees, just barely enough to land a helicopter and then lift it back out. One wrong move, and your tail-rotor would be in the branches. A corrective move from this situation and your main-rotor would be cutting leaves and small limbs. One thing that this training did teach me was smooth control. When you introduce cyclic control, whatever you put in to start the directional movement, some of it must be immediately removed. Therefore, small, smooth, controlled movements were the answer to the smooth flying of this machine.

In the years to come, I was to perform as an instructor pilot and standardization pilot, and I found out one thing—the slow-moving (not to be confused with the slow-thinking) easygoing, "laid-back" type of person made the smoothest pilot.

One point I want you to know about was the type of equipment we were using in our training. We trained in Bell helicopters, 47 E's and G's. They had the motorcycle twist-type throttle, so with your left hand, you kept the R.P.M. of the engine in the green, and at the same time, your left arm was moving the collective pitch up and down. Your right arm and hand held the cyclic control, and you never let go. At the same time, your feet and legs were operating the anti-torque pedals.

The turbine-powered models, which were to come much later, were a dream. You set up what percent power you wanted to use and pulled up the collective pitch and went. A fuel metering system took care of your requirement. So I got to do it the hard way, and then high tech came along, and I received the benefit from it. I got to do it the easy way.

As we were nearing the completion of the course, we transitioned to the H-25 helicopter. It was a twin rotor type, which they laughingly called a cargo helicopter. On a really hot day, with the crew of two pilots, they could carry a mechanic and his toolbox, providing the toolbox was not too large. One other thing that bothered me somewhat during the course was that we had contract maintenance. The contractor had gone out and hired a bunch of peanut farmers, given them toolboxes, and told them that they were mechanics. It was not uncommon to go through two or three machines before you found one that would check out as able to fly.

My instructor in the transition training was from San Antonio, Texas, and I will never forget him. He had a case of Lone Star beer sent to him every week. As soon as I was able to perform auto-rotations in the H-25, he said that I had passed the course. I did not fully realize what I did to make the machine do what I wanted, but the anti-torque pedals had a lot to do with its performance. They kept the back rotor from out-running the front rotor and changing the direction I was trying to maintain.

The last week or so after we had found out that we had made it through a very difficult course, which had cut our starting numbers by more than half, we were able to unwind, relax, and enjoy our last few days at Fort Rucker. We were upper classmen, who had completed all the required subjects and had been signed off as being qualified to be Army aviators——rotary wing. I had such a feeling of accomplishment that even to this day when I go back in my memories to that time frame, I feel good. Igor Sikorsky had just turned out a much larger, single rotor, cargo helicopter and most of my class were to go with me to Fort Sill, Oklahoma, to train in this machine.

The day came, and we got our wings and bars. As soon as it was over, we headed to Chattanooga, Tennessee, where Libby and I were to meet to get our mobile home, which my brother had used while I was in school. We bought a new pickup truck, hooked up the mobile home, and headed out for a new assignment in Oklahoma. Coming out of the mountains of Tennessee, Libby was fearful that the mobile home might outrun the truck. I was not sure that might be the case. We had a lot of weight on a half-ton truck, but the electric trailer brakes performed very well. We drove slowly, and soon we were out in the flat country.

Shortly after dark, we were both tired, and the important factor was that we had been separated for three months. We pulled off the highway, jumped into our bed that we were pulling behind us, and got a good night's sleep. As we were getting out of bed the next morning, there were some people standing there looking in the living room window at us. I guess they just wanted to see what the inside of a home on wheels looked like.

We were all trying to make good time to Fort Sill and get our families together and set up because our training was to start right away. A classmate of mine had driven all day and was driving in the middle of the night. His wife was sleeping in the backseat when he had to stop for gas. He paid for the fuel, went to the bathroom, came out, jumped in his car, and hit the road again. Fifty miles down the road, the state police stopped him and suggested that maybe he should go back and pick up his wife. It seems that when my friend was in the rest room, his wife woke up and decided she would go to the rest room also. At least she remembered the tag number and the make and model of the automobile, or my friend would have been on the road without his red-headed wife.

We pulled into Lawton, Oklahoma, and found a park where we could set our mobile home. The first thing the neighbors told Libby was that if you see a big cloud in the west to run and get your clothes off the clothesline, or you will have to wash them again.

They were right about this. There was one dust storm after another in this "Tornado Alley." They seemed to come close to us all the time. I did not see it with my very own eyes, but I did hear that one of these storms blew a three-pound chicken into a gallon jug. Sand was everywhere. It would somehow get into the bed between the bed sheets.

We then made a run to Texas and retrieved our children from the grandparents. We were a family once again, and it was great.

The H-34 helicopter, built by Sikorsky, was the top of the line helicopter in this time frame. Powered by a Wright radical engine with over 1,300 shaft horsepower, it was a dream. The Army maintained that it would carry a combat squad of men. It could do this, but the fuel load would have to be cut down. It would carry what I called a "sawed-off squad" a much longer distance, and this is what we would usually do.

If I remember correctly, it had a sling. We could pick up and move a 106 Jeep, which was the regular Jeep, with a 106-millimeter recoilless rifle mounted in it. If you got into trouble with the sling load, you could release the load and be free of it. I saw the result of this when a crew got into a bind and turned a 106 Jeep loose from about two hundred feet above the ground.

We completed our transition, and then went into company tactics to include formation flying, taking off, and landing at the same time with all our helicopters. We also did a lot of instrument flying. It was not that easy flying on the gauges on such an unstable platform as the helicopter, but we tried to learn enough about it so if we should get into the clouds, we had a chance to get back out safely.

Also, we found out that we were to be assigned to Germany as soon as we were up to strength with personnel and helicopters. This was a fun time for our family. Just about every other weekend, we would make the trip home to Texas to see the Texas grandparents. It is good we did that, because in short order we were to be stationed in Germany for a period of almost four years.

My unit was finally up to strength in personnel and equipment, and we received our marching orders. Poor Libby. Housing was not immediately available, so she was to follow later with the children. She went home to Texas to wait until we had a place to live.

We packed up and flew our helicopters to Mobile, Alabama, and put them aboard a baby flattop. It was an old *Victory* ship converted with a flight deck and hangar deck below. The ship was so top heavy that it seemed like it would roll even while it was still tied up in the harbor.

About one week out at sea, we hit a storm. I later decided, after many trips across the ocean, that there was always a storm out at sea. I could see why the old sailors preferred a hammock rather than a fixed bunk. I finally figured out a method to stay in the bunk. I would sleep on my stomach, hook my feet under the rail at the end of the bunk, and put my arms under the mattress, and the weight of my body would hold me in place. Well, most of the time it would work for me.

We docked in Bremerhaven and flew our helicopters to a little airfield just outside of Münich, Germany. I remember how beautiful the country looked from the air. Realizing the true value of their forests, the Germans very early developed the science of forestry and replaced every tree cut down with a young stripling. Our airstrip was located within a few miles of a small city of Dachau, which had been a Nazi concentration camp/extermination center. We were billeted within a few hundred meters of the ovens and the huge grave behind them. It seemed to still contain a strong odor of death. On a stormy night, with very little imagination, you could hear the wailing of the tormented.

Our airfield at Scheissheim had been used by the Luftwaffe and had been fairly well destroyed by the bombing raids. A few old hangars were still usable, so we set up our maintenance shop in one of them. There was a lot of underground area with tunnels going everywhere. One such tunnel was said to go all the way into München. They were cleared of demolitions and booby traps by engineers in years past, but I knew from my experiences that some might be missed, so I did not explore very far and was very careful about what I did poke into.

Each little village had its own brewery and made beer like their ancestors had made for centuries. It was great but treacherous. Some of it might be thirty octane, and the next thing you knew you were walking around on your knees. . . .

We got settled in and started some training and became familiar with flying in our area. We had been put on a list for housing when we got our orders, so all we could do was wait until some became available. Libby had taken our automobile to New Orleans to have it shipped to Germany, so all we needed now was a place to live.

One thing that really fascinated me was the road system. The Autobahn, as it was called, was a wide, four-lane road, which avoided big city traffic. There were no intersections, no railroad crossings, and no speed limit. Later on when we were driving on it, we would be doing about eighty miles per hour, and cars and trucks would go by us like we were standing still.

It had been built for safety and speed, and they were able to move a lot of equipment in a short period of time. This road system had been constructed prior to 1940 and was still in excellent condition, and this would indicate that maybe taking that lowest bid is not always the way to go. Also, it was built under a dictatorship, which would discourage the graft and corruption that plagues our system. They had very few accidents on their road system, but when they did have one, it would be a total wipeout because of the high rate of speed.

Motorcycles and bicycles were the basic means of transportation in the towns and cities, and they were everywhere. Young or old, male or female, everyone had a bicycle. During the rush hour, there were thousands of them, and they had as much right to the roadway as an automobile. They did not have horns, so we would intimidate them with ours to move them out of our way.

Good news! We finally had housing available so my family could join me. Libby and our children were on the way. She had gone to the saddle maker and had a harness made for each one of them. It had a long strap for each child, so she could pull them in when she wanted them. It was a great idea because our two kids were plenty mobile. Plus, she did not want to lose them during the trip.

She did really well. She got to New York City and got on a plane with eighty other wives and an untold number of children and came to Germany. Everything went smoothly, except she was one day early from the time that I was to meet her in Frankfurt.

When Libby arrived in Frankfurt, and I was not there to meet her, they tried to put her on a train to München, but they had never run across someone like this gal from Texas. She told them that her husband was going to meet her, and she was going to be there when he came. They told her that they did not have a room for her and the children to spend the night, her reply was that they had better find one for her. She put her luggage down, put David, who was four years old, and Sandy, who was two years old, on top of the bags and instructed them to scream if anyone came close to them. She went to change her money, and when she returned, the authorities had given in and found her a place to spend the night.

The next morning I arrived, thinking I was on schedule, only to find out they were already there. I got the room number and found them just coming out of their room to go eat breakfast. We had a joyful reunion in the hallway. We were to have many more of these reunions, and they were wonderful, but the good-byes were always so very hard. We were a family again, and life was great.

We had a beautiful apartment in the southeast corner of Münich. Our housing area was totally military and just across the street from our building was the theater. We could send the children to the show on Saturday afternoon and watch them go in and come out. We had a German maid, who cost almost nothing, so Libby decided to learn to play bridge and also how to smoke. Neither one worked out. She could not stand the small talk at the bridge table and almost burned the house down learning to smoke.

At the airfield in Scheissheim, we were a battalion-size unit with two helicopter companies, a battalion headquarters, and a maintenance unit to perform upper echelon type maintenance. We were in direct support of 7th Corps, headquartered in Stüttgart. We spent a lot of time in the field in support of various units involved in training.

Each winter found us in the field on maneuvers. We learned to cope with the bad flying conditions, cold temperatures, snow, and ice. The machines would have to be started up every hour or two to ensure that they would be available when we needed them.

A fellow pilot and I were assigned to fly the corps commander on alerts and field exercises. When the alerts were activated, we would get to the airfield as soon as possible and crank up and fly to Stüttgart to pick up the corps commander and fly as directed. My fellow pilot had a lot of helicopter time, and normally we would trade off on the flying and navigational duties, but I found out really quickly that he had trouble with the large-scale tactical maps, which we used to find a clearing in the woods. Most of his time had been as an instructor at Fort Rucker. When he got out of the traffic pattern, he was lost. So I made a deal with him. He was to do the flying, and I would tell him where to go. I did not think that our careers could stand getting the corps commander lost. We had this position for a long time, and it worked out well.

We fought the cold war all the time I was in Germany. There was one alert after another, so we kept the equipment ready and our bags packed. When we were called, we had no idea when we would return, as we never knew if it was a practice alert or the real thing. It was really difficult on the dependents, who had to keep a certain amount of food available and suitable clothes for a trip of several days.

Their bug-out plan involved using private vehicles and going by convoy to Switzerland. If it had been the real thing, I do not think it would have worked out because the German civilians would have known about it, and the roads would have been clogged with traffic. I heard that after we left Germany, they ran such a drill and even with normal traffic, they did not get some of the dependents back home for a day or two because they were lost. At the very best, it would not have been very good.

We usually kept two helicopters in a central location close to the Czechoslovakia border, and these were used for patrol along this border and further north in the East German border. Everyone had to pull this duty at one time or another. You had to learn your sector like the back of your hand. It did not run in a straight line, and there wasn't a cleared area to define the border. An accidental crossing would have caused all kinds of trouble. It was fun.

We would hover up to a point directly across from one of their observation towers and wave at them. They would point their weapons at us, remain passive, and keep us under observation. This would continue until we were tired of it, at which time we would give them the international high sign, drop the nose of the helicopter, and move smartly down the border.

We also kept a helicopter and crew on duty at the airfield for evacuation in the Münich area. There was always someone getting in trouble in the Alps. Lost or injured, we would try to find them or pick them up and transport them to the hospital. One such trip was to pick up someone, who was reported to have been in an accident. It was an Air Force officer, who was going down a mountain road in a toboggan and met a Volkswagen coming up the mountain. He was alive when we loaded him, but when we got to the hospital, he was gone.

There was also a man, who had gotten on a ledge of a rock on a mountain and could not get off. Bad weather kept us away for about two days, but when it cleared, we got to him. With just enough room to put one of the main gears on the ledge, without the rotor blades striking the side of the mountain, the crew chief got him into the helicopter. On the way back to München, the chief called over the intercom and told us the man was trying to drink the oil out of our oil can. He had been trapped for at least three days without water.

I had been designated as an instructor pilot shortly after our arrival in Germany, and this kept me busy. I conducted training and checked out new arrivals, which included two new battalion commanders who arrived and departed during my tour of duty. For one of these gentlemen, I could not sign him off as "qualified" to fly the machine. It did not seem to bother him one little bit that when he had to or wanted to go somewhere, I had to go with him. When we would come back from a trip, I would drop him fifty feet from his office. He would say, "See you later," and he would be back in his office in one minute. R.H.I.P.—— rank has its privileges.

5

W E GOT IN A LOT of valuable training in the mountains. Why not? The Alps were in our backyard and just minutes away. It was so beautiful; the valleys were so green and the mountaintops were covered with pure white snow. I fell in love with this country right from the very first day.

We were impressed by the German people. They are thrifty and industrious, and what really got my attention was that they also knew how to relax. They would sit for hours over their cups of coffee or glasses of beer listening to brass bands or a small orchestra, but the military is bred into them. I drank with them, and danced with them, and when they were in as bad a shape as I was, they would say America and Germany could rule the world. Think about that for a minute. I am very sure that forty-odd years have––well maybe not changed, but *outgrown* or *outlived* this feeling they had right after the defeat of the Third Reich.

We were very fortunate to be stationed in the state of Bavaria, the playground of Germany. We had many unique places to visit, especially the old castles that dated back in time by hundreds of years. Also, the Alps were so very pretty. Both in winter or summer, they attracted people by the thousands. We also would try to attend the Ice Capades in Garmisch every time they changed their program.

Then there were the outdoor areas and the forests. The German people were always out walking in their beautiful wooded countrysides. I always thought that if you went out in the woods at midnight and threw a baseball as far as you could, chances were you would hit somebody with it! They were really outdoor-type people, and their health seemed to benefit from it. The countryside was so beautiful in every season of the year, either white with snow or such a pretty deep green.

As an instructor, I was required to go to different areas to check out other pilots. On one occasion I spent some time in Nüremberg, the site of the international trials of the Nazi war criminals. What a thrill it was to roll back the throttle at one thousand feet and shoot an auto-rotation to a one-of-a-kind airstrip! The only one in the world, built out of granite blocks, where Hitler's legions marched and stood in review of the entire world. Had the military been given a free rein, it could have been in control of all of Europe. The German people, since back in the days of the Hun, had leaned toward the military way of life and the rewards that came from it. I would not say that the German people are war-like, but they are very competitive in anything that they do. They had great pride in themselves and their country, which was very much like we were at that time in history.

Since Vietnam, I have really had my doubts about my country really being able to go all out in a fight for our existence. The same people who marched in protest with our involvement in Vietnam would undermine us in our efforts. These numbers are still in our country, entrenched in every level of our society. Some of these people——I simply cannot think of them as fellow Americans——are nursing on the taxpayers to the fullest extent, like a parasite sucking the lifeblood from our nation. They gave nothing; they are taking everything, and no type of sacrifice was made by them, yet they could condemn our way of life and our goals.

Sometimes I wonder if maybe total freedom, in some way, is bad for our country. It is my personal opinion that if Grenada, Panama, or Desert Storm had encountered large losses in personnel, which would re-crank up the draft, these people would fall out of the woodwork once again. They would stage their demonstrations once again, and their offspring, who by now would be of conscription age, would begin their exodus to Canada and other parts of the earth.

Just maybe it could be that I really have not been as fair as I should have been with my one-person opinion of these on-and-off-again Americans. It could well be that if the invading forces were here established in our own country and had them surrounded, they might very well resist until their lives were gone. Decisions are made by our elected leaders and I believe that, right or wrong, we as Americans, should obey and carry out whatever their decisions dictate. Well, enough of that for now.

It was always such a pleasure to fly over Germany. Everything that we looked down on was orderly and neat in its patterns. Every little piece of land was utilized, like a jigsaw puzzle, with every piece in the proper position. We flew in all kinds of weather, both good and bad, and the bad was sometimes really bad. The unwritten law was when navigating by Autobahn, stay to the right side of it, or you might meet a chopper head on. I am talking about weather just barely clear of the clouds and with forward visibility almost nothing.

On one occasion, I was instructed to take a helicopter to Koblenz. After I had flown to Mainz, the weather went down to nothing. The clouds were in the treetops and forward visibility was non-existent. I found the Rhine River and dropped down into the river valley and just a few feet above the water, I flew up the river. I know that I shocked some crews on the river barges when I had to fly around them to continue up the river. It was very much like flying in a tunnel, with the water just below and the river banks on each side and the clouds just a few feet above. I arrived at Koblenz safely and put on a static display for the German people.

A day or two later I departed for my home base near Munich, and I flew back the way I had come, which was down the Rhine River. I could not believe what I saw. It was a day you could see forever. On my trip to Koblenz, I had flown under countless cables draped across my path. When I saw with my own eyes what I had done on the way up, it sent a cold chill down my spine. Another hair turned gray, and a hair, which was already gray, fell out. I made a vow to never do that type of thing ever again.

Libby and I made a trip on our vacation to Holland to see the Tulip Festival. It was great, and we were impressed with the Dutch people. Then we were on to Brussels, where the World's Fair was being held. We then went to Paris, France, where we stayed for a few days. We checked in at one of the better hotels and looked around at all the things to see, and there was so much to look at. We went up into the Eiffel Tower, but the clouds had the top covered up, and we could not see anything.

Back in our room that night, we were just about asleep when voices came to us through the walls. The man was English and the woman was French. The voices increased in volume. Neither one of them understood what the other one was saying, but it was very obvious that they were trying to agree on a monetary figure which was agreeable to both parties. I do not like to have to report to you that the love affair of the year did not come off because of the language barrier, but in a few minutes the door slammed and high heels went clicking down the hallway. Since Libby and I had no language problem, we got a good night's sleep.

On our departure from Paris, Libby had the city map and was doing the navigating while I was trying to dodge the world's worst and fastest drivers. After one hour of defensive driving at its very best, we were still in the city locking horns with the wild frogs, instead of being in the countryside where traffic would smooth out. Then I picked up on something. We had crossed over the same damn bridge at least three times. We had been traveling in circles. I immediately relieved Libby of her co-pilot duties and followed the sun until we were out of town.

We were happy to get back to Munich and see our children, who had stayed with Hilda, who was now like part of the family. In fact, wherever we were in all those military years, together as a family unit was home to us. Some other military families could not adjust to this and were miserable their entire tour.

Libby then came down with a sore throat and went to the hospital to have it checked out. She had the mumps, so we put her to bed and fed her soup. The next day when I reported to work, I did not feel very well, so I checked in with the flight surgeon, who sent me home. I told Libby to move over and make room for me.

No one wanted to be around us, except for a fellow pilot and his German girlfriend. They came and took care of us even though she had never had the mumps. What a wonderful person! May God bless her forever. They later got married––and are still married.

David and Sandy hugged and kissed us while we were ill, but to this day, they have not had the mumps. I only had them on one side, and later this was to cause me much grief on a presidential visit to a foreign country.

We made a trip later including our children. We went to downtown Munich to a shop that dealt with outdoor living. We purchased a small tent and everything else that we needed for camping out. Loaded down with food from the commissary, we headed out to Italy.

Out of the thirty days we were gone, we stayed in a hotel just one night. We went down the Adriatic coast and back up the Mediterranean coast, with all kinds of side trips into the inland. One trip was to the oldest city in that country. We also went to Rome to see where the Christians were thrown to the lions. We met a lot of people in the camping areas from nations all over the world. It was a fun trip, and our children enjoyed doing something different.

While leaving the Italian border, we had some Italian money left, so we stopped at a wine shop and showed them how much money we had. We told them to stop us when the money was gone. Libby picked the wine out. She did not know any more about wine than I did, which was nothing—well, this is not quite true. I did know that some of it was made out of grapes. Well, we ended up with our cast iron six Plymouth car just barely climbing over the Alps to get us back home to Germany. We gave wine to everyone that we knew and to some we did not.

It was fun living in a three-story building! Living in a mobile home had really not prepared us for this. People were below us; people were above us, and people were across the hall. Across the hall were Americans, and he was C.I.A. The people we were sure of were just below us and members of our unit.

The French people, who lived above us, invited us up to their place for drinks and to play cards. We noticed that they had an unusual cat that just sat there and stared at us. It was not long until we figured out that he would be doing that forever; he had been stuffed after he had used up his nine lives. He would have made a nice doorstop.

When you are young, you do dumb things. Well, even after you are older you still do, only maybe just not as many and not as severe. Anyhow, when the French couple would come to our house, I would load his drinks up because I thought it was funny to see him crawl up the steps trying to get home to bed. He would do the same to me when we were up at their place, and he would laugh at me falling down the steps on our way home.

David and Sandy very much liked their school and their friends. Surprising as it may seem, there is a close bond between young people when their parents are military; we all speak the same language.

When winter came with all its splendor, it would snow almost every day. The snow would be almost three feet deep. Whoever was unlucky enough to have to leave the complex early in the morning would clear a path to get his vehicle out to the main road. Then the plows would come by, and it would have to be cleared again.

Our son would blaze a trail on his way to school with just his head and shoulders appearing above the snow, and once in a while, we observed the blonde ponytail of his baby sister following in his footsteps. They would arrive home from school cold and wet, but happy, because of the pleasure of playing in the snow.

With the helicopters, we had to be extra careful with the loose snow. It was easy to stir up so much snow at a hover that we would lose all reference to the terrain. It was like being in the middle of a sugar bowl. If we got in that condition during a landing, we would pull pitch and climb out of it. Out in the field we had to be extra careful about where we set the machine down because the snow could cover up tree stumps, and as the machine settled in the snow, it would poke a hole in the belly.

It seemed like we always spent a lot of the wintertime out in the field on exercises, and it was miserable––always cold, and always wet. What a horrible combination! Years later, while climbing into a cockpit in Vietnam, with the temperature 120 degrees Fahrenheit, I thought about the wintertime in Germany and wished for some of it. Just goes to show that the human being is never completely satisfied with the present.

The last summer that we were stationed in Germany a fun mission came along. The Norwegian government requested helicopter support from our country in building a string of microwave stations on the mountaintops running the full length of Norway.

We took seven machines, plus a small support unit and went north. We flew the helicopters across Germany and Denmark and from there across the water to Göteborg, Sweden, and then up to Oslo. There we met the representatives of Norway, mostly military, who briefed us on our mission. We had a day or two to get our equipment ready for the long haul north, so we had a little while to look around.

What a wonderful city! Everyone had a job or a function to perform. There was no unemployment in this nation of three million people, who were so happy and proud of their forefathers and country. Of Teutonic origin, as were the Swedes and Danes, the Norwegians were the people who resisted the Nazi invaders. They were fun-loving people, who believed in the Almighty and in themselves. They had to be tough to endure the climate and the sacrifices made during the reconstruction of their country. I was so lucky to meet some of them. Most of them spoke English, since a second language was required in their schools, and most of them chose our language.

We were quartered at an Air Force base the first night, and we stayed with enlisted members of their military who flew the F-84's. What a group they were! When they said that they would flip you for drinks, look out. That night I learned to do my famous over-the-back-of-the-chair trick. You would approach the chair from the back, put the weight of your body on it, and without touching the floor, you would end up sitting properly on the chair. I would not attempt that now.

There was plenty of food to eat, but I had trouble getting my taste buds converted over to fish that was almost raw or tasted as if it had been kept in a brine barrel. So I ended up living on eggs and bread.

When our equipment had been serviced and inspected thoroughly, we flew north to our first work site. The material, which we were to carry to the top of the mountain, and the fuel for our machines, had been stockpiled at the base.

Nearly every piece of cargo was carried by sling. We would hook up a sling load and start climbing up the mountain, pulling about sixty inches of manifold pressure and climbing about two hundred feet per minute, depending on the amount of weight we were carrying. We would plan our route so that we would arrive at altitude and the top of the mountain at the same time.

We would drop our load, hover to the edge, and auto-rotate to the valley floor, then hook up, and start the climb once again. We kept our fuel load light so we could carry more cargo. Everything that was to be used on top had to be lifted by us since there were no roads to the top. We would fly until we were dog tired, and at that time of year, it did not get dark, so at midnight we could still be flying loads to the top.

I experienced difficulty sleeping as it was always bright as daytime, but I beat the rap by taking the bed covers and putting them over the windows to shut out the light.

There was a little house built on the side of the mountain about one-third of the way up. How they built it there I do not know, but we flew over it on the way up with the loads. On the way up, one of the helicopters had a partial loss of power close to the house and the pilot had to release his load of lumber. It looked like a handful of toothpicks floating down, and it just missed the house. The next day as I was hauling up to the site, I happened to look down and saw someone building a room onto their house. I guess he figured that the Good Lord had sent the lumber to him.

A Norwegian military officer went with us with a briefcase full *of krone,* and each day he would pay each member of our unit our per diem. We used this to pay for our meals and lodging.

My boss sent me ahead to the next site with some Norwegians to make arrangements for our meals and a place to sleep. What a ride that was! We flew in a single engine Norseman airplane equipped with floats. The weather was bad with very low ceilings, so the pilot followed the fjords with the floats of the aircraft only a few feet above the water, and he made steep turns when the terrain would suddenly change. It was like flying in the tunnel once again with a rock cliff meeting the water and clouds fifty feet above. There were no landmarks, and it all looked the same to me, but an hour or so later we arrived at Trondheim. I was really pleased to see the weather clear up for our return trip so we could see where we were flying. When we would finish one site, we would move on to the next.

I had noticed at the last site that there were two young blonde girls, who were on the top of the mountain where we would drop our loads of equipment. I did not think much about it until they showed up at the next site when we did. How could they get there so fast in such a rough country with very few roads––and not good ones at that? Well, I put two and two together and came up with the fact that someone in our group was giving them a lift in their helicopter when we would move to the next location. More power to them.

We kept working our way north and finished up at Hammerfest, a little city 300 miles north of the Arctic Circle, which was nearest to the North Pole of all the cities in the world. The Norwegians had sent drums of fuel by ship for our use and off-loaded them on shore. We would land at the fuel dump and refuel our helicopters. The mosquitoes were so bad that we had to keep one machine running to blow them away so our personnel could refuel.

The only industries they had were fishing, and the Laplanders had their reindeer herds. It was a raw and rugged country but so beautiful, and even though I was homesick for my family, it was with a little sadness that we flew home to Germany. The Norwegian government was very appreciative of our efforts and expressed that to our unit commander. We had finished our regular tour, and we were on an extension, so when I applied for another extension, the Army turned it down and gave us a departure date.

We were on our way to the States to see family and friends, whom we had not seen in almost four years. The Germans came to our quarters and packed up all of our personal belongings. With the usual efficiency that they displayed in all their efforts, they packed Libby's lunch while she was trying to keep an eye on the boxes and what went into them. She was able to retrieve her lunch about a month later back in the States.

We had the option of returning home by air or surface. I talked to Libby about it. "Hey, you have not been on a ship floating across the ocean. It will be like a cruise, which people pay big bucks for. Besides we will take the train to the P.O.E. and that will be something new for all of us."

If Libby would have had one inkling of what was going to take place on this trip, she would have told me where to go and how to get there.

6

THE TRAIN TRIP WAS A lot of fun. We had a compartment for the four of us with good food, a nice bed to sleep in, and excellent service. All we had to do was make sure that David and Sandy did not get off the train on one of the stops. When we arrived at Bremerhaven and got over to the port, we boarded the ship for our ride home. It was a good size ship, especially outfitted for the transportation of military personnel and their dependents. It had all of the comforts of home and then some. I was appointed Assistant Provost Marshal, which did not have much responsibility to it except to make sure no little ones got up on deck without their parents. We were settled in our compartment, and everything looked fine when Murphy's Law went into effect.

Sailors from the crew came around and started to secure all the hatches and portholes. The ship was untied and pushed out into the North Sea. What followed was nine days of hell for Libby and most of the passengers on the ship. It was rough, about two rolls and the pitch, which made sounds like the bottom of the ship was cracking.

When we got into the English Channel, it got worse, if that was possible. We pulled into Liverpool, England, for one day and a night, while we waited for the weather to get better. It did not appear to improve, so we headed out for New York. Libby had eaten one or two meals before she got so sick, so she did not want to go to the galley anymore. The rest of the trip she lived on crackers and cheese that I would bring her.

It stayed rough almost the entire trip, and the number of people who made it to the dining room got smaller and smaller. I know that it was a bad thing to have done, but I would walk into the dining room smoking one of my King Edward cigars, and people waiting to eat would head for the door, not to be seen again that day.

On one occasion, two grown men and I were sitting on a couch when we got a bad roll, and it broke loose, and we saved ourselves by getting our legs up and making a cushion against the other bulkhead. Some sailors, who had made that run for years, said that they had not seen it so rough for such a long period of time. Libby might deny this, but at one time when she was so sick, she said that if the children had not been aboard, she wouldn't care if the ship went to the bottom. Now that is *really* sick! I did get her up on deck one time to watch the *Queen Mary* or the *Queen Elizabeth* go by us. It was a trip that she would like to forget but will remember forever.

Years later I conned her into going fishing with me on a head boat out of Grand Isle, Louisiana, with the same results. It got so rough that they could not tie up to an oil rig, so we returned to land and for the first time in their history, they gave us our money back. Now when she talks about going on a cruise, I have to remind her how snake-bit she is in regard to traveling on water.

It smoothed out some for the last day and was nice when we arrived in New York. The Statue of Liberty was a welcome sight as it is to anyone coming in from the sea. I did not see her do it, but I am sure at some point after we off-loaded from the ship that Libby knelt down and kissed the ground. We got the location, where our automobile had been unloaded. We found it undamaged, and we loaded it with our hand-carried items and ourselves, and then we looked at a map and headed south for our country's capital. I had orders to report to Executive Flight Detachment, Davison A.A.F., at Fort Belvoir, Virginia.

Executive Flight Detachment was my new assignment, and I really knew very little about it and its mission. I did know that it was a prestigious unit in direct support of the White House. It was a very small unit, which made it even more select. I would wager that the reason I was sent to it was because of the high number of flying hours which I had accrued in the last four years in the very machine, which now was transporting our President.

We arrived at Fort Belvoir, and I signed in at my new duty station and went to have our name put on the post housing list. We found an apartment in nearby Alexandria, put our children back in school, and returned to normal family life.

It was a short period of time before I was privy to what I was actually to do. Background investigations were performed because I was to receive Top Secret Clearance and the much-coveted White House Clearance. Once this was completed, I found out what my duties were, and I started my check of the different locations and routes, which would be used for the duration of my tour in support of the White House.

I did not know at this time, or could even make a wild guess, how this would affect my life and the lives of my family. I also did not know at that time that the remainder of my career, with the exception of a tour in South East Asia flying for the Security Agency, would be flying in support of the White House. I think that not knowing what you will be doing in the future is the real joy of this life.

In addition to the Top Secret and White House Clearance, I would end up with a Crypto and Special Intelligence Clearance for my involvement with the Security Agency. There was not a war room they could keep me out of if I had business in there.

When I arrived at my new assignment, they were transporting President Eisenhower in a greatly modified H-34 helicopter. It was plushed up on the interior with plenty of sound-proofing to help kill the roar of the engine and main gearbox. It also had floats on the gear that we could inflate if we saw we were going to make a water landing. Top of the line communications were installed so the President was always in touch with the people he might have a need for. The top part of the helicopter's exterior was painted white, and it was identifiable almost as far away as you could see it. We had two of the fully plush machines, so if one was down for scheduled maintenance, one would still be available for the President. The rest of the ships were semi-plush with the exception of one, which was just plain vanilla to carry the baggage in.

We had a partner in this White House helicopter business, since the Marines had the same type equipment. It was set up to alternate trips with the President, but both Army and Marines pulled the standby duty jointly. Our standby duty station was in Anacostia Naval Base just across the Potomac River from the Washington National Airport and two or three miles from the White House. Our route to and from Fort Belvoir was fifty feet above the river. This let us in and out of our duty station under the air traffic operating at Washington National Airport without upsetting the airline people.

It also allowed us to operate in marginal weather because once we got over the river, we would just follow it. Our counterparts, who were based at Quantico, just a few miles down the river, would use the same procedure to go and come to their standby duty station. They were the Jarheads, and we were the Doggies. We were very competitive in our duties, but over all we got along really well. We had to.

We lived together for forty-eight hours at time in a ready room. We passed the time playing poker, reading, watching the latest movies, and sleeping. We never knew when a drill would be called, and not knowing if it was practice or the real thing, would keep anyone from resting well.

Our ready room was on the second floor on a Navy hangar with our helicopters parked just outside on a flight line. When the bell went off, the race was on. We flew down the ladder, through an engine room, and outside to the machines. If it occurred during duty hours for the Navy, they soon learned to clear the way for us. I would guess that after being knocked down and run over by the stampeding horde, anyone would have to be pretty dense not to get the message. Now and then, a newcomer would get in the way, and down he would go. There were many cuts and bruises, and I also remember a broken leg, but I cannot remember whether it was them or us.

The Navy had ways of getting even with us. They had about fifty C-45 aircraft parked on a big ramp just outside our ready room, and shortly after sunup, they would run the engines on every last one of them. The roar of the engines was deafening. You could not talk on a telephone, listen to the TV, or anything else. If you would let it, it could give you a headache.

But one morning the brakes on one of the aircraft failed. The aircraft jumped the chocks and chewed up two or three of the others in front of it before they could get it shut down. That made it quiet for a short time while it was investigated and new procedures were implemented.

On the drill, the first member of the crew to get to the cockpit would begin the starting procedure. As soon as we could, we would engage the rotor head and bring the RPM up. When we had sufficient RPM, we would lift off, jump over the river dike, and the race was on.

When we crossed the Fourteenth Street Bridge, we would call our White House control on the radio for instructions. Everyone strived to be the first to call in, so I am sure we cut some corners on the safety end, but we felt it was justified by the importance of the mission. At least we justified it so in our minds, and anyway, it was our butts that were hanging out.

As I think back to the cold winter months, we would run up the machines every so often so they would not be dead cold if we had to go. We jumped over the dike and headed up the river without a single instrument in the green except rotor RPM. If the engine had coughed one time, the results would have been a swim in the river. After we received the turbine-powered machines, it was neat. Once we got the fire lit, it was rock and roll time with no cold engine to worry about.

We would pull our two-day duty on standby, and then return to our home base for a day or two off duty. We would then have training for a day or so on our routes and sites, and then we went back across the river for standby duty. Now and then a trip would come up to break the monotonous duty of the ready room.

President Eisenhower did go to Camp David nearly every weekend and that was nice. The crew that was flying the chase ship was invited to take their families. That was super for the wives, as they were waited on the whole weekend. There was a bowling alley, and there were movies to watch. The President liked westerns so we saw plenty of them.

I did not see it with my own beady blue eyes, but I heard it from reliable sources, both Army and Marines, so I am certain that it did happen. A Marine chopper on a recon mission to Camp David had landed on a lower pad and was fixing to lift off when something had a malfunction, and the helicopter rolled over on its side and beat itself to death. No one was hurt, but the aircraft was badly damaged.

Now, normally we would fly the President into the top pad, but in doing so, all he would have to do was look down at the wrong time, and there, for the whole world to see, was the wounded bird lying there. At the time of this incident, the President was due to arrive in one hour, so this triggered Marine ingenuity, and they acted promptly. A bulldozer was at hand, so a temporary resting place of the dead bird was prepared in the earth. The mortally wounded helicopter was pushed in and covered with dirt to be retrieved and salvaged at a later date.

Quarters became available on post, so packing and moving was the order of the day. Our children were pulled out of school and away from newly made friends. It seemed to be a raw deal at the time for them, but now I believe that it enriched their personalities and made better adults out of them.

It was great to be living back in the military environment, where everything that we might need was available almost within walking distance. Also, it was great to have neighbors who knew everything about you, and who would, in time of need, do anything to help you.

Libby fell into her role once again, and besides being a wife, lover, mother, and a good friend, she was a den mother for our son, and she helped our daughter, who was in the Scouts. Plus, our son had a paper route, and that meant he rolled out of bed early to hit the trail on his bike and throw papers for his route. This was not accomplished without the aid of someone, especially in inclement weather. Since I was gone so much of the time, this "someone" was Libby. Army wives, like all service wives, should receive a special award of commendation. Better yet, maybe they deserve a head start on their wings to be used in the final kingdom.

Somewhere in this time frame, we made an overseas trip in support of the President. As I look back now, I cannot believe what we did. We operated and looked like sharecroppers instead of acting like the chosen few that we really were. We were to supply the President with helicopter support at the Summit meeting in Paris, France.

We flew our machines down to Norfolk, Virginia. We folded up the rotor blades and tail-rotor pylon, where they were picked up by crane and deposited on the hatches of an everyday, plain vanilla freighter bound for Roto, Spain. We had special covers made for the helicopters to protect them from the seawater. Helicopters are basically made of magnesium, which really comes from seawater, and they just cannot wait to return to that state through the process of corrosion. With these special covers made for them, we were hoping that this would not occur. In any event, as soon as we could, we would wash them down with fresh water. Anticorrosion control was practiced by our unit on a full-time basis because of our proximity to the salt air, where we were stationed.

The ship was loaded to capacity with ammo and bombs for General Franco, who was Chief of State and Commander in Chief of the Armed Forces with dictatorial powers. We rocked and rolled across the ocean without any air conditioning, and as I remember, the food was not the greatest. Also, the always present storm was brewing somewhere in the crossing, but we finally reached land, and we were in Spain.

We off-loaded the machines, and put them back into flying condition under the watchful eyes of the Spanish police. What quaint looking people they were with their three cornered black hats, their very colorful uniforms, and their old-time rifles. We were airborne once again. What a way to really see the country at treetop level! We could watch the chickens scatter in every direction on the countryside. They must have thought that we were giant chicken hawks about to swoop down and grab them up.

We flew across the country, which was not unlike our southwest. There was nothing but scenery, which appeared to be very unproductive, arid, and unpopulated. We landed in Barcelona and spent the night. The city was in a festive mood, as the bullfight of the year was being held there, which is much like our Super Bowl.

General Franco had come to town with part of his Air Force. Lordy, what a ragtag looking outfit that was! A sharecropper's delight, dating back to World War II. They were in aircraft that was so obsolete it had been discarded by the major powers. At the airport, where we parked our machines, it was like being in an air museum of a war that had been over for fifteen years.

We checked into a hotel that was in the heart of the city. What a mistake that was as not much sleep was to be had that night. People filled the street and music floated on the sound waves from dark to dawn. The next day, on the way to Paris, the crews took turns flying and sleeping.

Arriving in Paris, we secured our machines and equipment, checked into our living quarters, and with a few days off before our mission, we hit the bricks to tour the city. Pig Alley, look out, here we come.

It was, at this time, that I discovered the subway. It turned me into the original tunnel rat. I could look at the map at every station, figure out my route, and pop up out of the ground exactly where I wanted to be. My comrades spent their money on taxis, but I moved merrily along underground, and it cost me hardly anything.

With only one day to go before our President would arrive, and our mission would begin, a terrible thing happened. It would shock the free world, the Intelligence Community, our military, and most of all Gary Powers, sitting in his U-2 seventy thousand feet above the earth, where he probably thought that God was the only one who could touch him. He was brought down by a Russian missile. That was the excuse they used for not attending the Summit meeting. So arrangements were made for our return home.

They did have a big parade for our President in Paris, and some of us were standing along the street on the curb when the President came by in an open car. We snapped to attention and rendered the hand salute; he returned it, and as he drove away, he turned back to look at us and gave us a wave of his arm.

Our business was completed. Crank them up, pick them up, and move them out. We said "adieu" to Paris as we flew through southern France and down the coastline of Portugal. What a picture that was with the old wooden boats that the fishermen used. It seemed to take you back a hundred years in time.

Arriving in Lisbon, our C.O. came up with, what turned out for me, a bad idea. Just one officer would accompany the enlisted men and the machines back on a ship, and the rest would fly home. Damn those cards. Why did I have to draw the deuce? Well, it was the fair way to select who had to rock and roll back across the ocean. Maybe.

I had a day or two to look around and take in a bullfight. I cannot remember whether they killed the bull or just cut off an ear. Anyway, this would have driven the "save the rattlesnake" people nutso. We ended up loading our helicopters on a "reffer," which was a refrigerator ship, which had just come out of the Mediterranean Sea from replenishing the Sixth Fleet.

Helicopters were tied down on the deck and covered for protection from the elements; equipment was loaded, personnel boarded and were counted three times. How in the world would I explain to my boss how I left one of our people in a foreign country? There was no justification for this worry. Our people wanted to go home just as badly as I did. We just wanted to get the hell out of there and get the show on the road. We wanted to be back with our families and with the people who talked like us and with food we liked and could eat without being sick.

They had a problem with me as to where my billet would be. All the officers' quarters were filled with the regular complement. Even though I would have liked to have lived with the enlisted men, because in my heart I was still one of them, I was assigned to the sick bay. There was no problem with staying cool, as this ship was one big refrigerator.

Time passed slowly, like it always does when you have nothing to do. I let a naval doctor talk me into having my warts removed, so that was the big event of the day. He would pour some liquid fire on them each morning, and in ten days they were gone, and they have never reappeared. Thanks, Doc.

They had it set up so that we could shoot skeet on the deck. So every day I would sharpen my shooting eye. I read a lot of books, watched some movies, but the best time I had was below the deck when I talked to Libby over the ship-to-shore radio. The procedure of the ship-to-shore was explained to her. You talk, pause, and use the word "over" to signify termination of your conversation. But what was not told to her was that saying, "Hurry home and I'll jump your bones," was heard by the whole world.

Being back home again was great. It seemed like I had been gone a year instead of a month. I did not have to wait until the machines were off-loaded and checked over because I was told to head for the house. Other members of my unit would do this, and I could get back to my family. The children had all grown an inch or two, and our baby daughter had changed so much, like they all do when they are below the age of one year. I heard all the stories of what had happened to them, both good and bad, while I had been away this trip. They were all happy to see me, even John Paul, our miniature French poodle.

I was back in the swing of things with going across the river to pull standby duty training and flying routes to the bug-out locations. Not many trips were made because our President was finishing his second term. His life-long duty to our country was nearly over, and his well-deserved rest was about to begin. What a man this was! It was almost as if he was not a mortal being, since he reached the very highest pinnacle in the military and then went on to serve as our President for two terms. This person should go down as the greatest American of this century. When he was finished with this service to his country, he had so little time left to fish for trout and play golf.

President Kennedy took his oath of office and became our new boss. Our duties changed very little at this time, except more travel was performed by our unit, and we saw change in the faces of our passengers. They were much younger in age and full of energy, and some of them were pumped up with the knowledge that they were very important in the White House circle. Most were very polite when we would fly them to different locations, but now and then, there would be one who would turn out to be a pain in the you-know-where. Usually we would find out that this person was in the very outer ring of this White House circle.

I enjoyed flying the Press Secretary, Pierre Salinger, because we both smoked cigars. He favored those, which cost a dollar, and I made do with those which cost me the whole sum of one nickel. Either he was forgetful or he did it on purpose, but he would leave one of those expensive cigars behind when he off-loaded.

It was a fun time, and a real change from the former tenants. Everything was kind of jived up with the young and smart running with the ball. It was one of those "world at your feet" things, where they could do no wrong. President Kennedy was swept into the highest office by a majority of voters of this great land. The lifestyle does not change overnight, but optimism does prevail. A Democratic administration has a habit of giving so much hope for the betterment of life in the beginning, and then it turns sour toward the end of their term. Come to think of it, the other party has the same results.

It had been funded and approved. We were getting new flying machines. It was the twin turbine SH-3A Sikorsky helicopter, a real dreamboat with 1050 horsepower from each of the G.E. turbines. A few of us were sent to the factory at Bridgeport, Connecticut, for our check-out on the new machines, and then we were sent home to check out the rest of our pilots.

Shortly after this, I had the honor, along with my boss, Colonel Jack Tinnin, of flying the President for the first time in a twin-engine helicopter. We picked up President Kennedy from the South lawn of the White House and flew him to Atlantic City, New Jersey, and we then returned home to the South lawn. He stopped by the cockpit on his way off and told us how much he liked the machine and the flight. He more or less warned us that he would be giving us a lot more business, which was an understatement if I ever heard one.

He was a mover with a lot of trips, both short and long ones, which included the West Coast. About that time, the missile crisis with Cuba came up, and we ended up in Florida. He wanted to talk to the troops, who were on alert status there, so we were needed. It was a very dramatic time frame because just one incident could trigger the third world war and could signal the end of civilization on this planet. But the Soviet Union backed down and withdrew the missiles from Cuba. They may have realized that it was a no-win for either side. This would give us enough time to watch our children grow up and maybe see some grandbabies. (Or so I thought––but another war was to come, and lucky me, I was to have a ringside seat.)

We made a lot of trips back and forth across our great country with President Kennedy. They were real fun, and I was really impressed with our President. He was always very polite and always stopped by the cockpit to tell us that he enjoyed the flight. I truly believe that nearly everyone loved him and what he was doing for our country.

Another over-the-water trip was to come our way. The President was to visit Germany, Ireland, and Italy. As it is usually the case, the more you do a certain thing, the more efficiency you gain, unless you are as dumb as a post. This time we did not fall into that category. This time we were not acting like poor kin-folks. We were traveling in style with a baby flat-top vessel. The Marines used it as a helicopter assault platform. It was complete with a flight deck and an elevator down to the hangar deck. Besides the Navy crew and a Marine security unit, there was just us, the chosen few. We were up-town, traveling in style.

We had the packing of our equipment down to a science. Like most bands of gypsies, we knew what to take and what would be left behind. Our machines were flown onto the flight deck, blades folded, and then down to the hangar deck. Boxes of supplies were stowed and personnel boarded.

One of our crewmen was not feeling well and, after an examination was found to have the mumps. No one was too eager to be near him to get him off-loaded. What the hell! I had already had the mumps, so we packed his gear, and I carried his bag and got him off the ship. This was to haunt me later and put me in one of the most miserable positions I have ever been in.

Under way again, this journey was to be made in solid comfort with very nice living quarters and topped off with the best food. The Navy knew how to live and were outstanding hosts. We had smooth sailing with only one day and one night of rough weather. Like every other trip I made, we had to hit a cattleguard somewhere during the crossing.

Fifty miles off the shoreline of France, helicopters were made ready. Crews were selected for the various assignments, and the gear was loaded aboard the proper machines, and we were ready to go. Lock and load. We were on our way with another Presidential mission in Europe. I was going to Germany for a day or two and then on to England and Ireland. We refueled at one of our bases in France, and then we were on to Germany. I was in my second home again. It was great. Everything was so familiar, the people had not changed. The hard-working, fun-loving, honest people with character were still there. I loved every bit of it. It would have been so wonderful to stay a few days longer––but it was not to happen.

We cruised across the lowlands, with the countryside looking so neat and clean, as did the canals, which carried the bulk of their commerce. Finally, over the last dike and the English Channel, there loomed in the distance the White Cliffs of Dover. They really do look white, probably the aftermath of the birds that roost upon them. The countryside of "Merrie old England" appeared below us with the little villages and the roofs of thatch. It appeared that each living soul had in their possession a two-wheeled vehicle, better known as a bicycle. It was a very pretty sight. The fields were small but very green. It somehow looked like a darker shade of green from what I had been accustomed to.

We tree-topped into a small airfield somewhere near London where we spent the night. The crews were loaded on an old bus-type vehicle and taken to our billets. Our arrival there coincided with the arrival of a storm and darkness. People met us at the bus with umbrellas to keep us from getting wet.

The inn reminded me of what we have all seen in the movies––a poor man's castle and not extremely large. I could not hazard a guess as to the century it was constructed, and I truly believe it would look sinister even in the sunlight. The interior was dimly lit and a musty damp odor prevailed. We were shown our sleeping quarters, which were adequate. Well, anyhow, we had beds. The dining room consisted of a large long table, which we could all get around. I could not identify the main course, but it had a smell of sheep. A restless night was spent. The storm continued on and off during the night, while the ancestral spirits had a ball dragging heavy chains around and slamming doors and shutters. Boy, was I ever glad to pull up the gear and be airborne for Ireland!

We flew into Dublin on the *Emerald Isle,* and from the air it was beautiful. President Kennedy wanted to visit the site of his ancestors, so we ran a recon to the area. As I remember (and that was a long time ago), it was located in the vicinity of Limerick. It was nothing more than a stone house with a few out buildings, which were most likely several hundred years old.

When the President arrived in Dublin, we picked him up and flew him to that site. He looked into the old buildings, talked to some of the local residents, and then we took him back to Air Force One. That was it. He was on his way elsewhere. At least, he was able to see the origin of his roots and how his forefathers had lived. It was well worthwhile, as not many people make it back to the exact location where their bloodline lived and died.

We were to stay another day in Dublin before heading out on the next leg of our mission, so we had a chance to walk the streets of this city. In later years, I was amused to see the commercial on television advertising Irish Spring soap. They must have exported all that they made because the people that I had contact with that day did not use the product.

I would have loved to have visited some of the ancient ruins which stand as silent witnesses to Ireland's past glory, but duty awaited. Maybe someday, before being called to the big hangar in the sky, my bride and I will make that return trip, and at our leisure take in the pleasures of that very pretty country. Out of the land of the leprechaun, where the grass is truly a deep dark green, and into the early sunlight covered by the clear blue sky, we were on another leg of our journey.

With the flying Dutchman, Vietnam 1968

Vietnam 1968
In front of a makeshift bunker

Barney Hulett piloting the Army's presidential helicopter
on the south lawn, circa early 1960's

Picking up new aircraft at Bridgeport, CN at factory.
Sikorsky helicopter 1962 Barney Hulett at top of stairs.

President Kennedy was the 1st U. S. President to be flown in a twin turbine helicopter. He flew from the south lawn to Atlantic City and returned back to the White House. 8 May 1962

Barney Hulett is piloting aircraft

Campaign trip, Pocatello, Idaho, early 1964,
Barney Hulett in pilot seat.

The author waiting in the cockpit as the President,
First Lady and Secret Service prepare to board
the helicopter at the Texas White House.

Lyndon Nugent --- Barney Hulett
Texas White House

Last A/C we had before retirement
(LBJ Co.)

Three former First Ladies prior to flight
from LBJ Ranch to Dallas

Barney and Libby Hulett with Mrs. Lady Bird Johnson in living room of Texas White House LBJ Ranch House.

The former President Johnson's grandson, Lynn Nugent (left) and the author at the LBJ Ranch in the early 1990's.

7

WE SET OUT ACROSS THE Irish Sea and into England for a refueling stop. After lifting off, we saw the English Channel and the very pretty low countries slide along below us. Landing in France just before nightfall to refuel once again, we learned that the French controllers had found out about our mission and decided they would not work that night. Those dang Frogs are something else! With the help of some radar from the bases we still controlled in Frogland, and with a nice clear flying night, we pushed on to the outskirts of Rome, Italy.

Now during this little junket of one day and night, I had not been feeling quite up to snuff, but I chalked it up to a cold and not having had enough rest. The main symptom was a very sore throat, plus an overall run-down feeling. Upon our arrival in Rome, and finally getting to our new home-away-from-home, I noticed a pool with nice cold water. Now, maybe the devil made me do it, or the fever in my body took over what common sense I had left, but the result was that I went swimming in that nice cold water.

In a few hours, I was to pay for this folly. I was deathly sick, and my seeds of manhood had enlarged to the size of a citrus fruit in the orange family. I was in much pain and needed relief, and this was complicated by the fact that we had no military in the area. So this is how I ended up in the Catholic County Hospital in Rome, Italy, and had a little peep into what hell really is.

The first few days passed rather quickly as a result of my high body temperature, which induced a sleep of sorts. They gave me medication of some kind and plunged me into cold baths and kept me covered with cool wet cloths to try and get my fever down. I really do not know if what they did was proper or not, but I began feeling well enough to look around and see where I was.

It appeared to be a very poor hospital, not in the care that they gave, but in the fact that they had little money to operate on. It was a noisy place. The people, who worked there, would bring their children to the hospital with them. Maybe some of them even lived there. No one spoke English. They had not yet invented ice, and the food—when I finally could eat—tasted like it had come out of a brine barrel.

My comrades had thrown a small radio in my personal belongings when they committed me to this hell on earth. I could receive Radio Free Europe on it, but with my luck, the batteries faded in a day or two. An orderly popped in, a man who tried to speak English to me. He let me know that he had been a P.O.W. in the U.S.A., but if he had learned some English, he had forgotten most if it. I asked him if he would please bring me something to read. He brought three issues of *Life* magazine, which were about five years out of date. I thanked him very much and memorized every one.

About this time, I received a call from the Embassy telling me that my unit had departed the country and that they would see to the arrangements for my trip home when the hospital released me. That was the kicker—getting loose from this cuckoo's nest. I asked the Embassy to coordinate my release from the hospital since they could at least speak the same language.

I was told, that by their law, anyone who had a communicable disease could be kept off any commercial carrier for thirty days or more. I replied, "I do not give a you-know-what! I just want to get an airline ticket back to the real world." I was back to the drawing board.

Hospitals are fine when you are sick, but the very minute that you are feeling better, they become your prison. The person at the Embassy could sense my disappointment and asked if I needed anything. I ordered ice cream, and it was delivered to me. It was the very first cold item that my body had received in days and days. They delivered one gallon, and I ate every bite before it turned to soup.

At the very start of my incarceration, I remember that every morning five or six little boys would enter my room, line up in a row and stand at attention and salute me, while saying, "Buon giorno, Americano," and then they would giggle. I had the last laugh. As I was leaving there, two or three of them had come down with the mumps.

A few more days of waiting, and I received the call I had been waiting for. They would allow me to depart their country on a commercial carrier. Hot damn! I was soon to be back in the real world and united with my family. The day came, and the voice from the Embassy, which was next best to hearing from God, informed me of a departure time and that transportation and the proper paperwork would come to me. This voice, God bless him, wanted to know if I would like a tour of the city on the way to the airport.

I replied, "NO! NO! NO! And please, just in case the driver does not speak English, inform him that I would like to go directly to the airport."

I could not take the chance of missing my flight. I had to escape from Devil's Island and return to my family. I could not take a deep breath until the feet of the big Iron Bird came up. I had experienced a very small taste of what a P.O.W. would undergo by being confined to an area where no one could speak your tongue and being separated from family and comrades. This is probably a very bad comparison, but, Lordy, was I ever glad to depart this part of the world and this time of my life.

Our tag-along daughter had been born during this administration while we were stationed at Fort Belvoir, Virginia. She was a late joy to all of us, especially to a sister who was eight years older, who had been born in Texas, and a brother ten years older, who had been born at Fort Campbell, Kentucky, while I was in the paratroopers. This should tell you something about Army life. I was to be reunited with my lovely family, and life was great.

I was back in the routine once more with stand-by duty for the White House and the occasional trips around the country with the President. We were in the fun mode and rockin' and rollin' along, but then the day came when our existence was gruffly shattered. Every American of the age of recollection knows exactly where they were and what they were doing on that dark day in our history.

It was our counterparts, the Marines', turn "in the barrel" as we called it, and they were with the President in Texas. I was on a training flight in the Virginia area and to make the flight a little shorter, I listened to the local radio station. This was broken by a special news broadcast. Shots had been fired at the President's motorcade in Dallas, followed by the President having been hit. A short eternity passed and then the facts came. Our boss was gone, killed by black-hearted cowards in an ambush. This day and the new President and his family would forever shape and influence the lives of me and mine.

Back at the airfield, I waited for orders. Like most military units who had been called back to duty stations, we sat in solemn silence. What in the hell was this? Was this the beginning of an attack on our country or a lone act of a few insane people? Orders were received—report to Andrews A.F.B. with three of our helicopters.

The new President had been sworn into office and was en route to the capital city aboard Air Force One. Upon his arrival, the body of John Kennedy was carried and loaded into the hearse. The widow insisted upon traveling with the body of her husband, and they were gone into the darkness. President Johnson made a statement to our country calling for calmness and unity. He then on-loaded our helicopter for the short flight to the South lawn of the White House. We had a new "Boss."

Very little time, if any, was lost in the transition to his job, as President Johnson hit the ground running. A special commission was appointed to investigate and come up with all the facts, and possibly some answers, on how and why this, the darkest day of my lifetime, had occurred. Later on, the findings of this Commission were generally acceptable to the citizens of our nation. As the years passed, new evidence and conjecture has sprouted up to cloud my feeble mind and the minds of others as to the authenticity of the Commission. There is a possibility, and it grows larger as the years pass, that we will never know the truth of this tragedy.

Back in the routine once again, our mission remained the same, even though we changed bosses. We were on stand-by duty for possible evacuation of the White House because the cold war was still in full swing. We conducted trips across our land because election year was at hand, and training was never ending. We were the elite unit and an accident or even an incident could not be tolerated. The one new activity, which jumped out at us, was the trips to the Texas White House. It seemed like Pres. Johnson spent just about every other weekend at his ranch in Texas, and yes, all of the big holidays, too.

Election year came and went with the nomination received, and the voters giving their consent. Then it was down to business with a bill on Civil Rights and Education, and it appeared to be easily passed but not so. I am sure that arm-twisting was involved. The fact that President Johnson had been the Senate Majority Leader before becoming Vice President, helped much more than it hurt. He knew where all the bodies were buried.

Halfway around the world, in a country few people had even heard of, the rattlesnake had coiled up and was ready to bite us. The number of troops and support units had slowly increased to maintain the sovereignty of the South. Pacification was a failure, and advisors to the ARVN were not getting the results they had planned for. In fact, the Cong were eating their lunch. This had to pull some of President Johnson's attention away from his domestic issues. Under all the stress and strain of running the country, plus the fact that we were digging the hole deeper and deeper in Vietnam, put a heavy load on his back. He needed to relax when he could, and he found a way to do this. He loaded up the essential personnel and headed for the ranch for a working weekend.

We would be in position at Bergstrom Air Force Base awaiting the arrival of Air Force One. When it touched down, it had a long taxi to a secluded ramp area, which was under tight security. The doors would open, and the stampede for the helicopters was in progress. It was a known fact that if you were riding with the President, you had better be in the machine first, or you would be driving the eighty miles to the ranch. As the Boss came aboard, the door followed him, and we were pulling pitch at the same time to make like giant chicken hawks into the fading sun. Before arriving at the Texas White House, he always wanted to check out some of the ranches that he had, so sometimes it was a big race with the setting sun.

Prior to this, we had performed a reconnoiter of all these ranches and selected safe landing sites. To assist in landings during darkness, we had outlined the site with rocks painted with a fluorescent material. Then all that was required was to be in the vicinity of the site and turn on our powerful landing lights, and the landing area would stand out like the proverbial prostitute in church. We also had navigational headings from any one site to another, because the Boss would not do anything in sequence.

A lady passenger once remarked that in our tour of the outlying ranches that she could not understand how a Ford Bronco was always there to meet us even though it had only required a few minutes to fly to the new site. Little did she know that the Secret Service had three such vehicles.

Another jaunt was to the lake, which was later named for the Boss. After landing at the lake house area, the Boss and his friends would jump into his boat and speed across the lake trying to lose the spooks. However, the Secret Service had the fastest small boat known to man at that time, so it was all for naught, but it took his mind off the problem of the war in Vietnam, and it was momentarily relaxing.

Now that this President was entrenched in a four-year term, unless bad health or some more nuts were out there to repeat what had happened to the previous President, we were fairly well assured that we would be flying down and back to Texas on a regular basis. We were putting high time on our machines going to and fro.

I don't know who to give credit to, but someone in a high position finally said, "Why in the hell don't we just transfer two machines and the crews to Texas? Then we will not have to fly down there every other weekend." A big high-five to the brain that came up with this! If the truth were known, it was probably a clerk in an office somewhere who did not receive a reward for saving our country a lot of money.

Well, anyway, as soon as I heard about this, my hat went into the ring. Boy, it would be so nice to get back to Texas, and of course, prayer does work, and soon we were on our way back to Texas. We bought a brand new house in San Antonio, put the youngsters in their new schools, and we were in high cotton.

Everything was new to this family. The children in their new schools made new friends and really readily adapted to their new environment. Being Army brats, all of their lives, was paying off big time now. We had a new church, which meant meeting and making new friends, and some of these friendships are still in place some thirty years later. It was a fun time because I was home more.

We operated out of Randolph Air Force Base, which really screwed up people's minds since we were in the Army. Gone were the forty-eight hours of stand-by duties for the White House. I worked fairly regular hours. We usually knew in advance when the President was coming home for a visit. We would be in position to pick him up and fly to the ranch. We would not always fly him there, as he would sometimes come in a smaller aircraft and fly directly to the ranch. In that case, we would position our helicopters at the ranch and remain there, at his beck and call for the duration of the visit. We would also be responsible for some of the Presidential trips in the Western half of the country. But all in all, my home time was much improved, and my family was enjoying life and having fun.

As a unit, we would make periodic flights in our area to locations that we could be called upon to fly the President. This included the closest place that qualified for minor treatment and of course, Brook General, at Fort Sam Houston in San Antonio, which could handle any emergency.

In our spare time—if and when we had some—we improved our home away from home. We had a mobile home set up at the north end of the runway with our helicopters close by on a ramp area. Reading, playing cards, sleeping, and watching movies killed hours of boredom. This would be broken by a radio or a telephone message to wind up the rubber bands because the Boss wanted to go somewhere. Sometimes we did not know our destination until he was in the machine, so we had to know the local area like the back of our hand. We surely did not want the lightning to come down and hit us just because we were not on a direct route to our final destination. Some actions cannot be forgiven.

While at the ranch with President Johnson, we would receive our orders from a military aide, who happened to be the pilot of Air Force One. This is really unique so let me give some background. He was passed over twice as Captain in the USAF, and of course, I do not know for certain that this happened, but his superiors must have been looking for him and pushed him back in the corner, but somehow he ended up flying the then Vice President of the USA. Well, the Boss always surrounded himself with his "can do" people, and this officer was a "can do." Years later, I had the distinct honor to fly former President Johnson to this officer's retirement at Bergstrom Air Force Base. They directed our aircraft right up to the reviewing stand, and my Boss only had to walk a few steps to the VIP area. This "can do" man was a well-deserved retiring General in the United States Air Force.

Also, at the ranch was the White House Communications Group, made up of personnel from all three services. The President could be in touch with anyone, anywhere in the world. Also, the Secret Service was present, along with the Boss's personal physician. We were a small but close-knit unit, with only one objective—to serve our Boss, the President of the United States. Each unit had its on-site supervisor plus more bosses in Washington, but very little if any supervision was needed. These men were professionals, the cream of the crop and highly dedicated to their job. We referred to ourselves as the ranch hands.

The President was going to a conference in the Philippines, the exact site being Manila. We received our marching orders to get ready, and pulled out our list of supplies and support that was needed. He would be visiting other countries in that part of the world, so our needs would be extensive. Our boss in Washington arrived at the scene to oversee our preparation. We were going by air. Boy howdy, I was impressed because the last two overseas trips had been by surface vessels. No more dreary drawn-out days at sea for this cat. I was moving uptown. We would be using C-133's, AAF cargo aircraft with the rear-loading ramp. This required removing the rotor system before loading our helicopters.

The day arrived and our equipment was loaded and tied down. The ramp was up, and our seats were installed in the ramp area, where we could strap in for take-off and landings. I was just a little suspicious when I overheard the cargo master remark that this was unusual because the Air Force had a policy of only the crew flying on the aircraft hauling cargo. After take-off, truth reared its ugly head. We had vibration, which is inherent to some degree in all helicopters, but not like this. I truly believe that if you stood on a newspaper on the catwalk, which is under the wings, that someone could slowly pull it out from under your feet. This was only part of our problems. After refueling in Honolulu, our aircraft did not check out, so we were there one night and part of a day fixing whatever was wrong with it.

In the air once again, our next stop was Wake Island. We pumped it full of fuel again, went out to the runway, and lined up on the center lines with throttles forward. I know we were past the take-off point when we aborted and the brakes were applied. I really did not think we could get it stopped in time, but we did—just barely. When we made our turn on the very end of the runway, all I could see was Pacific Ocean. It seems that when it came time for the water injection to cool the engines for more torque, the system failed, so we went back to the drawing board. While this was being repaired, we sat under a palm tree and drank beer. To avoid some of the vibration, we would sit in our helicopters and play poker. The struts on our machines would absorb some of this vibration, plus our machines were pretty plush with soft seats on the interior.

Finally, we arrived in the Philippines. I was tempted to rush off the aircraft and kiss the ground. It had been a very trying flight. We off-loaded the machines and equipment, and we began putting them back together again. The people at Clark Air Force Base pointed out a mountain about forty miles to the northeast of the base and advised us to stay clear of this area. The Huks, a guerrilla-type organization supported by the Communist party, were in control of that area. People went in and did not come back out.

We took a little side trip outside of the base in a Jeep borrowed from the Air Force. It was an eye-opening experience. People and dogs alike were going through the garbage piles looking for something of value or maybe something to eat. The country was being run by Ferdinand Marcos, President of the Philippines. From my viewpoint, the country appeared to be suffering from an economic weakness. Poverty was widespread, and when you saw someone who had money, they appeared to have plenty of it. It was really discouraging to travel on the ground in this land.

The helicopters were back together and test flights completed, so we could make our dry runs of the routes we would fly the President. After his arrival, we picked up President Marcos and flew the two Presidents to Rice Institute, where they were in the process of improving the quality and yield of rice. It was located about forty air miles south of Manila. Then it was off to Corregidor Island, which controlled the entrance to Manila Bay. There was a lot of history here. Corregidor was one of the last forts to fall to the Japanese in World War II. It had been defended by American and Filipino troops, and it was like a ghost town now. There were some old rusty coastal guns in place, and gun placements were falling down and rotting away. You could smell death in the air. I hope by now that it is a national park, where visitors may walk and see and feel what I did. It is a part of our history as well as the Filipinos'. Many American lives were ultimately cut short in this struggle to aid these people, and it should not be forgotten.

What must have been the best kept secret of all times came about because even we, who knew everything that was going to happen, did not know this. The Boss saddled up Air Force One and went to Vietnam to confer with his commanders in the field. From the Philippines, we scattered to the four winds. I took one helicopter and crew to Malaya (now called Malaysia), and landed at Kuala Lumpur. I think that in this time frame, they were still under the protection of England.

While they were putting the helicopter together, I ran the recon of the site we were to fly the President. I flew in a British helicopter, with two British commandos armed to the teeth, to a rubber plantation about sixty miles from the capital to approve a landing site. There was unrest in this country also, so no one went into the jungle without some cover.

Before we left on this trip, I had been talking to a poker-playing friend who was the on-site supervisor of the White House Communications at the ranch. He was always on the advanced team in all trips. "Where are you going on this trip?" I asked him.

With a big belly laugh, he informed me that he had a bye on this one, and he would be home with momma.

I approved the landing area, and as the pilot was getting his rotor speed up for lift-off, a person suddenly appeared out of a bamboo hut at the end of the landing site, waving his arms like a windmill. My poker-playing buddy wanted a ride back to town. I never did let him forget this day. On all other trips I would say to him, "Are you staying home with momma?"

We were staying in a tall, round building, unlike any building I had seen before or since. We were on the top floor with an excellent view all around us. The day before the Boss was to arrive, a group of people staged a demonstration at our billets, probably because of our involvement in Vietnam. Anyway, we had a ringside seat on top of the building. It was serious business but fun to watch. The police arrived in military-type vehicles and out of one of them stepped one of the largest men I had ever seen. He was at least seven feet tall with a beard down to his chest and a white turban on his head, and he was wearing a military-type uniform. He very much looked like Punjab, who watched over Little Orphan Annie for Daddy Warbucks. He reached into a vehicle and came forth with a thick, ten-foot pole that appeared to have a boxing glove on each end. He then moved into the crowds knocking the "you know what" out of anyone who got in his way. By the time he reached the building, the riot was over.

The Boss came and went. The mission was slick as a gut, and we were done. We had people in Bangkok and Seoul to support the Boss, and when we were all finished with our missions, our boss from Washington made a decision, God bless him. We were not going to have to ride those damn shaky transports back home, so travel vouchers were issued for commercial carriers, and this group returned home in style.

I was always happy to get home, and at this point, although I will admit that it was nice to travel to new places and see something new, but still, when we were heading back home, I could not wait to arrive there! I was back in the real world and back in my own environment with my loved ones, and back with people who liked or disliked me, but anyhow, I was back, and it was great.

Back at the ranch, we assumed our regular duties, and since the President came home quite often, we were kept busy. The anti-war nuts were getting more vocal in the newsprint, TV, and radio and with their demonstrations. One particular newsman hung out over in the lake area, where at times we flew our Boss for a little R and R. He had the unusual name of Smith. One day as we were taking the Boss to the lake, he remarked, "I want you to get me in there without Smith seeing us. Fly like they do in Vietnam," and then he added, "I hope I don't have to send you boys over there to learn how."

I looked over at my partner, and he nodded his head. We dropped down into a ravine and flew just barely above the rocks in the bottom, cutting the leaves out of the treetops, and if he was looking out of his picture window, he would have been looking up at the trees. We never heard any more about this.

Another time we were flying the President to one of his ranches, and when we touched down, he came by the cockpit and said, "Hold them in here for a minute." "Them" was a mixed group of men and women.

He then went down the ramp, undid his pants, and relieved himself on the ground. What he had maybe forgotten was this big picture window and that everyone inside the aircraft could see every move that he made . . .

It was an interesting time. We did everything we could think of to please our Boss. We would be rewarded with either a bouquet of roses or a cactus. There was no in-between. He believed in loyalty and that was the key word. He expected loyalty and really did not demand it, but he knew when he had it. No words would be spoken, but he could sense that fact, and in some way would let you know that you were a member of his team. We had become knowledgeable of the President's family and also his close friends because we flew them so often. It appeared to me that the President's firstborn was very much like her father, both in physical characteristics and personality.

We would land at the ranch and because everyone at that location would know of our arrival, the golf carts would come zipping out to meet us. They were driven by family members, who had preceded us, or friends, who arrived to spend the weekend with the First Family. Worst-case scenario was looking out of the cockpit and observing the carts being operated by ranch hands.

Arriving late one night, he stood in the doorway looking over our greeting committee, and the Boss turned to his firstborn, who was directly behind him, and asked her where her sister was. The reply that came back was something like this. "How in the hell would I know? I've been on this damn helicopter with you!" I loved her from the start.

The Boss would be invited to a neighboring ranch for dinner parties or other events. After we flew him there, we might wait for hours to return to the Texas White House, but one thing was for sure, we knew we were not forgotten. Food would come to us delivered by employees of the host.

The war in Vietnam was escalating, and more and more units and their support were being sent there. Some more heavy news was dropped on me. I received a reporting date for that location. The hard part would be saying good-bye to my family. I knew that as a soldier, a man who was making the military a career, that was what I had trained for, and I wanted to do my share. Maybe, all service people should be single, but even single people have family ties. To go one step further, maybe the Army should be staffed with orphans. Just kidding.

I got on with health shots, weapons firing, and a run-through of the Vietnam village where we saw how the Cong and NVA booby-trapped items. Lectures were attended telling us what to expect; financial matters were taken care of; an up-to-date will was made out, and I was ready to depart.

Then I received my orders. *What was this?* I was back to ranch duty. I found out that one of the replacement pilots had flown the Boss to one of the ranches, and he landed in some new cut hay, and when take-off time came, he could not develop enough power to lift the machine because he had sucked hay into the air inlets. He must have been a city boy. Anyway, he was relieved of his duties, and someone was told by the Boss "to get them other boys back."

Can you believe that the officer who had performed this dumb stunt was later the aviation officer for the whole Fourth Army?

My sleep-in secretary, who is also my best friend and the mother of our children, (and my wife for fifty-three years), and I were just talking about this time in our lives. It would have been so much easier to have been gone at this time than to have received a reprieve. My family had already had a mind-set in regard to my being gone for a year, but the Good Lord has a plan for each of us, so it was not meant for me to go to the other side of the world at this time. He was saving me for later——the Tet offensive. He was really going to put me to the test.

Ranch life rocked and rolled along while we ranch hands performed the same duties as before. There were maybe a few more trips here and there as the next year was the election year, and appearances had to be fulfilled. It is interesting to note that of all the time the First Family spent at the ranch, I cannot remember a "family only" time. There were always people coming and going and staying both day and night. What a terrible price for this family unit to have to pay! Just having someone watching every move that I made, around the clock, would have sent me into la-la land.

On the plus side, there were the instant cars, regardless of where we landed. Also, the Boss dearly loved to jump into one of his two Lincoln convertibles and drive around his ranch. As he drove out of headquarters, the Secret Service was right behind him. When he reached the gate, one of his automatic gate openers from the car behind would open and close the gate. When he wanted refreshments, they would come from the tag-along vehicle, and now and then you would hear over the radio, "Boys, throw that rock out of the road."

He also had a private aircraft and a civilian pilot, who lived on the ranch, but he did not use it much because of security reasons. It was parked in the hangar surrounded by hay bales. The pilot, who has since gone to the big hangar in the sky, was in charge of certain projects at the ranch. I should have stored that little bit of information in the back of my mind. The story was told that when the pilot returned from vacation, he found that all the out-lying buildings had been painted a light green color, a special paint made in San Antonio and later called LBJ green. The new painting also included the pilot's private mobile home.

Another item, which I had noticed in my many days spent at the ranch, was the elaborate communication system that was in place. As it should be, the Boss was able to get hold of anyone anywhere in the world, but then his fetish with communications really kicked in. Most of his private vehicles had radios installed in them, including his private aircraft. When he wanted to talk to someone, he wanted to do it NOW. No telling how many radios were plowed under the ground in the farming areas of the ranch by the real ranch hands. No one escaped the big loop cast out by the Boss. If he had lived to see this age with mobile phones in vehicles, fold-up phones in your pocket, and calls to and from a satellite, he most certainly would have been in hog heaven.

During this time, we were exposed to so many people, some rich in wealth and power, but so poor in traits and quality. It might have been about this time that I started to evaluate my fellow men more closely. After being in the presence of a person, sometimes for only a short period of time, right or wrong, I came to a conclusion about them. Unless I thought that in some way this person was contributing to mankind, and I do not mean by just paying taxes, I found that I could look right through them. Rich and powerful people can be parasitic, but by and large, most of the people we were dealing with and flying here and there were very nice.

Well, the time had arrived, as I knew it would. I was back to the real Army, not that I had not been in the Army all this time, but because of our mission and who we worked for, we enjoyed a certain status among our peers. Along with this, came some of the privileges maybe denied to others. I had really enjoyed being a member of this small, elite unit for so many years. Serving three consecutive Presidents, two of whom had departed to the big White House in the sky, had been a pleasure, an honor, and a whole bunch of fun.

I had temporary duty for a few weeks in the northeast part of our country at the security agency's school to learn a new trade. I was back home for a few days finishing up paperwork, receiving health shots, having a bon voyage party given to me by my old unit, and then it was good-bye––again. It was so difficult and painful to say good-bye to my family. It is very hard to do when tears as big as horse turds are running down your cheeks. Then I was into the big iron bird to chase the setting sun, and I finally arrived in the land where I was to spend the worst year of my life––Vietnam.

8

I CANNOT THINK OF ANY GOOD words to say about Vietnam. Some other words do come to mind—hot, humid, dirty, insects, poverty, and that smell of large-scale death.

We had just landed north of Saigon. If I remember correctly, it was called Long Binh. Anyway, the runway, which was built and manned by Americans, was large enough to receive a large aircraft. We off-loaded and filed into a large metal building for processing. As we were going in one door, there was a long line of troops in front of another door. They were waiting to fill the seats on the aircraft we had just vacated. Shouts of "You'll be sorry!" came from the outgoing group. Hell, I already knew that.

We spent the night in the replacement area in small tents with cots and mosquito netting at no extra charge. It came with the tent. During the night, we were hit by rockets, which was a helpless feeling because we had not been issued weapons, and it sent us running to the sand-bagged bunkers. Thank the Lord that it was not followed by a ground attack.

One year later as I was leaving from that same location, we were again hit by rockets. It ran through my mind, "What damn good did I accomplish on my tour?" Helping to send thousands of them to Buddha had not changed anything; they were still capable of throwing rockets down on me.

The next day I caught a ride in a truck to Saigon. Riding in the open back of the vehicle, passing through hundreds of pedestrians and people on bicycles, which I was convinced contained some Cong, made the hair stand up on the back of my neck. I would not be issued any weapons until I arrived in my unit, and it was a very uncomfortable feeling. Our headquarters were in Saigon, with units in different locations in Vietnam. I met my boss and was told where my duty station would be, and I was told a few details of our mission. A pilot from my new unit had flown down to pick me up and fly me to my new home. *Good Lord, this aircraft only has one engine!* I thought. I had really been spoiled by flying for the White House, but this was just the first step in returning to reality.

I had orders to stop at Cam Ranh Bay and contact our unit there. They threw me into a much larger aircraft, and I spent eight hours over Laos and North Vietnam. Then we went up to Da Nang, which was to be my main base of operations for the next year. I was met by another pilot who took me on a night mission for three hours. This concluded my check-out. All this was completed in a twenty-hour period with no sleep. Welcome to Vietnam.

Da Nang, on the coastline of the South China Sea, was not too many air miles from North Vietnam and less distance yet, to the west, was Laos. This was a rugged highland area, with the Annamese chain running northwest and southeast through this area, and in the year to come, I was to know this piece of real estate, along with many other pilots, like the back of my hand. The sprawling air base was southeast and almost joined the city of Da Nang. Protected somewhat by the China Sea to the east and the Bay of Da Nang to the north was the home of flying machines from all of our branches of service. Day and night were the same with war planes departing and returning from their missions. The roar of engines was almost ceaseless. It is no wonder that to this day, I have a high frequency loss in my hearing capability.

Some metal hangars were present but not many, and these were used for performing maintenance on the aircraft, but we sharecroppers were not allowed in this hangar. We had sandbagged revetments, and we worked in the elements. On my arrival, I found that the pilots were quartered in a villa in Da Nang with the promise that low rent housing was being constructed for us on the base. This could not happen fast enough for me, as our exposure rate was high driving to and from the villa.

On the job, our basic tool was a twin-engine aircraft with antennas sticking out of wings and other places. It looked like a porcupine and flew like a truck because of the added drag. It had a beefed-up tail section because in our business, we were required at times to make level rudder turns.

Oh my, if my very first lady instructor could see me now! She would have eaten out my "you know what." This type of flying was contrary to everything that I had been taught. But we found out that if we never flew in a straight line and made turns every two to three minutes, we were much better off. This was another bad habit that was hard to break back in the real world. But just maybe, it was the real reason that I was able to return.

I was immediately thrown into the briar patch by being informed that I was in charge of operations, and I also was appointed Standardization Instructor Pilot (or S.I.P.). They had been having problems with losing engines, and I found out that with the power setting they were using at sea level that they were getting a boost condition that was of detriment to the engine. We came down on our power setting, and things were better.

Due to the small number of aircraft and the large number of missions, I was forced to give check-outs to the new pilots while actually conducting a mission. It was a rare treat when I could take them out over the China Sea and give them a real check, which included some engine-out training.

Under my operations hat, I selected the crews for all missions and with the blessings of my boss, I made some changes. Just prior to my arrival, they had lost an aircraft on an I.F.R. flight. Maybe it was due to hostile fire or maybe failure of the aircraft, but two young pilots, who had not been in country very long and who had low flying hours and experience, took the backseat man with them to a fiery death. In selecting crews, I would put a gray-hair with the new man, and the gray-hair would be in command regardless of rank. You had to use every trick you knew, even stack the deck, to make a profit in this business.

I would like to say a word about this tropical paradise; it was hotter than hell most of the time, starting with it being 120 degrees Fahrenheit in the cockpit when we climbed in. You would never get cool until you climbed to altitude, and in the month of October, we received forty inches of rain. Our feet started to web, and everything else either rusted or mildewed.

Then there was the smell of shit pots burning. We had outdoor latrines with barrels cut in two to catch the feces, and when one was nearly full, we would pour diesel on it and burn it up. The natives would take this same product and put it on their fields to grow vegetables. This wonderful aroma drifted over the land and finally killed your sense of smell.

Days of the week were lost. There were no weekends to look forward to, no game of golf, and no outings with the family. It was get in the air;

go find them, and get them started on the trail to meet Buddha. There usually was not a reason to ask a person his rotation date because if you looked closely, you would see it stitched in his clothing, usually on the back of a flying cap with the day, month, and year that this soldier hoped and prayed that he would return to the real world——*if* he could stay alive until then. This fact was something to look forward to, and it became more important as your time in country grew shorter.

A mission would begin by reporting to the war room one hour before departure for a briefing by the XYZ personnel. They would tell us what they hoped we would get for them and the last known location. Priorities were handed out, and we were off to the aircraft. Weapons were checked. I was never without my weapon; I ate with mine; I slept with mine, and went to the latrine with mine. We also took an ax with us in case we went down, and there were survivors. They would use this to break up the Crypto equipment before burning the aircraft.

Preflight was completed, and it was into the clear, cool air. Our Dink-hunting trip was in motion. Our navigation equipment, for precise pinpointing targets within fifty meters, would precess so we would have to fly over a known object about every thirty minutes and update our system. We learned really fast not to use the same one more than twice, as they would be waiting for us. Our enemies were not just coming out of the Stone Age. They were smart and dedicated, and they adapted to everything really fast. They learned hard lessons and came back to overcome them. I often wonder if we had been in their position how well we would have fared.

Back on the ground once again, our position had not changed very much. They were still trying to kill us. We would get the intelligence reports, and they would not be hopeful. We would pull guard duty for our villa in case they decided to hit us. One night such an action took place. We had an ARVN APC, equipped with a mounted 50-caliber machine gun, located at the end of the street overlooking the entrance to our villa. The Cong crawled undetected up a covered ditch or sewer and killed one of our two Vietnamese guards before the ARVNs realized what was happening. They then reacted and blew them to hell, which is where they go after they are full of holes.

When we came out to go to breakfast and then on to fly, the bodies were still lying there waiting to be thrown on a truck and taken away. We were able to drive through this mess without driving over any corpses. It was not fun and games. This was real, and dead was dead––and it could be us or it could be them. I was determined that it would not be me. I had a family who wanted me to come back to them.

Shortly after this incident, the housing on base became available, so we got the hell out of Dodge City. Built of wooden construction, by the firm who offered the lowest bid, it was not much, but we were closer to our work. Now we had to put up with the rocket attacks. Downtown we were immune to rockets because they were afraid they would hit their kinfolks, but now they would hit us anytime they felt like it, and that is just what they did.

Any spare time that we had, which wasn't much, was utilized filling sandbags and putting them on the walls on the outside of our building. The third estimate people constructed a bunker for us, but we had to sand-bag it also. We kept working on it until we had about five feet of sandbags on the roof. We were lucky it was not put to the test while I was there.

I got to know that bunker very well. The last week before rotating, I moved my cot out of there and slept the nights away. I had made it this far and was counting on getting back home in one piece. The 122 mm rockets would come in on us and out would go *Puff the Magic Dragon,* a large aircraft, loaded for bear, with enough guns to supply a cyclic rate of fire of six thousand rounds per minute. It was a sight to behold. With every fifth round being a tracer, it was like Fourth of July. Plus he put at least one round in every square foot of ground. *Puff* would be directed to where they thought the rockets had come from, and then they started having some fun.

We were to receive two R & R's during our tour. Mine came up, and I elected to go to Hawaii. Arrangements were made, and I met Libby there. It was so nice to be with her! As time grew short––and it did in a hurry––we knew that we would be saying good-bye once more. She would be going back home to care for our family, and I would be returning to that hellhole halfway around the world. We did not know if we would ever be together again, so it was harder than ever to say good-bye. We vowed we would return at some time when we could both leave on the same airplane going home. In later years, we did just that.

Back in the briar patch once again, business was picking up. Pressure, put on the President and his advisors by the anti-war nuts, had stopped most of the bombing in the North, and it cost us many more casualties. The MIG hunters were still going up North. They had to keep them off our backs.

The morgue was set up on our side of the field, and day and night the *whap, whap, whap* of the helicopters could be heard, making their delivery of body bags. It was sad knowing that the bulk of these bags contained very young men who had not yet tasted life. I would have liked to have exchanged the contents of these bags and filled them with the anti-war nuts back in their safe schools. These were the people who kept our country from making the big strike and getting it over with. I really could not see the big picture, but I could see the results. One thing I do know is until the day I meet my Maker, I will not forgive these people. Some things are unforgivable.

A small village lay just outside the south perimeter of the base. We had been protected somewhat by a minefield, which lay between us, but a B-52 had gotten into trouble, probably with hydraulics failure, and elected to land at our base. Anyway, they could not get it stopped. It plowed into the field and blew up. So part of the mine field was removed, and this caught the attention of the Dinks who moved back into the village.

At night, as our war planes would be taking off over the village, you could see tracers coming up to meet them. The commanding general finally got a bellyfull of this and decided to burn it up. It was the show of all shows. The planes would take off and dump everything they had on them. With hard turns and still being in the traffic pattern, they would land, load up, and go again. They made crispy critters out of everyone and everything. Yet, a few nights later, as I was watching the aircraft depart, guess what, out of the rubble came the tracers. Tells you something, does it not?

Bob Hope and his troupe arrived. I got to see them get off the airplane, but I could not stay for the show. I was on my way out to the trail in the west country. It was not a trail with just one road, but maybe five or six that were used to move supplies down from the North. These trails were completely covered in areas by the jungle country. The B-52's would hit them, leaving craters big enough to put a house in, and the next morning we would see that the damage was erased with traffic moving as usual. Now we know that thousands of people worked all night to smooth out the holes. Most of this was accomplished with shovels and rakes as their use of bulldozers was limited because they had very few.

It was amazing what they could accomplish with such primitive tools, and they were becoming more brazen in their actions. We caught a dozer and two trucks with personnel in a valley in broad daylight repairing a road. On a discreet frequency, we rang up the fast movers, who had a ball dispatching this small group of brave but very dumb people.

We were now trying to find large units of regimental size, so we knew that things were heating up. Larger units were present and Khe Sanh had been under attack for many days, but the Marines were holding on. We kept aircraft in the air almost day and night for this one. More rockets and mortars were being dumped on us at the base. When we could find time, more sandbags were filled and put around our sleeping quarters. Of course, we could not stand a direct hit. There was no way to put sandbags on the roof of a temporary building that was barely standing under its own weight. So when the crap came in, it was an individual choice to run for the bunker or gut it out. Some individuals could sleep through it all but not me. I think I could hear them in the air before impact.

Our unit supported a Christian orphanage located at China Beach, and it was a real treat for me to hop in a Jeep and take our donations to them. Little children are the same everywhere in the world. They were always glad to see me and take the candy I had picked up for them. Now, all these years later, I wonder if the reason we killed their parents was so we could have our very own private orphanage.

Not very far south of the base was an area that was the responsibility of a South Korean Marine unit, where all its members were over six feet tall and very tough. They looked like they could kill you in a heartbeat with their bare hands. I talked with one of their officers at an intelligence briefing and asked him why they had so little trouble in their sector. He told me that when they were assigned there, they went and moved everyone out, burned everything, and then carefully screened everyone and everything that came back in. They had very little—if any—trouble in their area. They had the Cong out of their midst. Just maybe too much goodness flows through our veins.

It is so easy to say, if we had done things differently, we would have saved lives. Lives that are long gone now and remembered by their loved ones and, I am sorry to say, very few others. This of course, excludes the men and women who served there, whom we will remember the rest of our lives.

One day with a few minutes to spare, and we surely did not have very many, we went to eat at the Jolly Green Giant club and mess. On a pathway leading to the club were these giant footsteps painted green. This was the stomping ground of the most decorated unit in Nam, and if they were not, they should have been. Every aircraft monitored the emergency channel, so we would know of those in trouble.

For example, an aircraft was shot down in North Vietnam with the pilot alive and surrounded by Dinks. His wing mate was using everything he had to keep them off of him. The call to the Jolly Greens had been made. On their entry to the rescue area, they were shot down, and the call went out to get another "Giant" out there. I hope and pray they got everyone out. I was low on fuel and had to leave the area. My hat is off to these people and to those in this unit who are still alive––I salute you. Without this unit, whom we knew would come into the badlands to get us if we were down, it would have been so difficult to point the nose north bound.

One night as I was returning an aircraft, which had lost its radios, from Ph Bai to Da Nang, while downwind in the traffic pattern, I heard a sound followed by the aircraft going into a roll. I thought that I had been hit with a Sam missile. After getting the aircraft under control, I looked down and all the dock area was in flames. I was told that an LCT, unloading 155mm howitzer shells, had blown up. Eighty-five men were vaporized in an instant! Maybe a sapper, maybe sabotage, maybe an accident, but a lot of souls went upward together.

Not much time was available for us to have any fun, in such a grim background, but one time we did. As I remember, we traded whiskey to the Marines for poncho liners, and then we traded the poncho liners to the Sea Bees for a box of steak. We cooked them in our backyard, so to speak, and a great big bellyful time was had by all.

There was fellowship present here. We depended on each other to get us all home safely to the real world. The most macho person would become humble and obliging under the circumstances in which we existed. We flew in all kinds of conditions because we knew the enemy did not stop his operations merely because it was raining with low ceilings. As a matter of fact, that was the time he wanted to make hay.

One night we had a high priority target, and it was pouring rain down by the buckets, and the clouds extended to the moon. My boss went with me. Let me tell you, doing flat level turns in the soup with the instruments going crazy will put you to the test––but we got him.

A lot of missions were going on with a lot of aircraft in the air, and it was almost impossible to coordinate each one and have direct control of each aircraft from a central point, so you really had to keep the eyeballs moving to avoid mid-air collisions. One day while working away, an F-4 Phantom dropped out of the cloud deck just above us in a tight turn combined with a pull-up. All we could see was the bottom of the aircraft, and it was close enough to almost read some printing on the machine. I do not think he saw us––or if he had radar, maybe he was in the process of avoiding us. Either way, it was too close for comfort, and on my head, another hair turned gray.

Another day, but in the same area, a pair of F-4's were working over a target in support of a ground unit. On one run into the hot spot, one of the aircraft must have taken a hit because he did not pull up after the drop, but flew straight ahead into the mountain. There was no ejection, just a ball of fire. It made me sad to observe this terrible thing, but can you imagine how his poor wingman must have felt?

In wartime, bad things happen. Accidents happen also. I remember one morning, while driving around one end of our two parallel runways, a warplane landed. He turned off the active runway and was waiting on the taxiway for clearance to cross the other runway to his revetment area. As I got abeam of him, the canopy blew off, followed by the backseat man being shot into the air about seventy-five feet, but not high enough for his chute to open. It was tough enough to survive any mission, but to have returned safely to the home base and then for this to happen was double tough. He may have reached down to put the pin into disarm and somehow fired the ejection system.

Sometime during this time frame, someone with a warped sense of humor gave us a U 1-A, which was designated the *Otter,* like the water animal. It was a single engine, referred to as the *Ugly 1-A,* which looked like a box and flew like one. When the Army bought it, it was to be the answer to the transport of troops and cargo in a frontline area. It did have a short field capability, but once filled with fuel and cargo, it would only climb at two or three hundred feet per minute, and the air speed was slow, slow, and really slow. I remember that when we were using it back in the States, we would drive the air controllers nutso, because of the slow air speed and rate of climb. They would get mad at us because we were really messing up the flow of traffic, and they would end up vectoring us off of the airways.

If you had any kind of a flight, you had better take a box lunch with you. We were not going to steal any business from the Air Force with this machine. It was reliable, but awkward to fly on approaches to the runway with a stiff crosswind. You had to crank in a lot of rudder trim unless you had legs of steel, and then just before touchdown, the wind usually played out, and then you were busier than a sick cat covering up you know what, trying to get the trim out so you would not be cross-ways on the runway.

Anyway, back in the land of fun and games, I immediately checked the records to see who the lucky person was. I just knew that in all the talent that I had, that there was an *Ugly 1-A* driver. Guess what? They were also smart enough to have gotten it taken off of their records. All but me, so periodically I would make supply runs down to Qui Nhon for parts. I would zoom out of Da Nang at eighty-five miles per hour and fly feet wet over the China Sea to Qui Nhon, which was also on the coast, pick up the parts and speed back home. After returning from one of the runs, they counted twenty some holes in the aircraft, and the only thing I remember flying over was some junks, which appeared to be fishing, who might have cut loose on me, or maybe it was some of our people, who thought we were too ugly to be in the air. Well, it was flying——but just barely.

I had used my long R & R up when I met Libby in Hawaii, and I use the word "long" loosely because it seemed so short in time. However, I was offered a short one, three days in duration, to be spent either in country or in Taiwan. I would have gone to Iceland before spending three more days in this hellhole called Vietnam, so I chose Taiwan.

The day came. A charter air carrier came into Da Nang to take over one hundred of us out to a half-real world. At least maybe they would not be trying to do us in, and we could get a good night's sleep. He took off to the south and stayed low and did not make a left turn to get over the China Sea as we always did. I reached for my flak vest to sit on, but of course, it had been left behind. What in the hell was this fool doing? This was not a sight-seeing trip! Finally, he started a climb and made his left turn. We had gotten away with this dumb stunt.

The man sitting next to me was a Marine, and we started to talk. It came out that he was the sole survivor (or maybe one of two), who took a direct hit on a bunker. This poor Marine was going away for three days and then back to the crap. He should have been on his way home instead. I hope that he did make it back to the real world.

Three days in Taipei went pretty fast too. I found a place to eat within walking distance from my hotel that was geared up to feed Americans. A fast food delight, which tasted almost like McDonald's. I ate all my meals there, and one night after walking all over Chinatown, I went to a picture show. It was not in English, and there were no subtitles, but I enjoyed it. I laughed when they did and cried when they did. I almost felt human again, but it was to end, oh, so soon.

I was on an airplane with a ticket labeled Da Nang, which really meant hell. I will never forget those days and nights when it was so peaceful and tranquil. It seemed like only minutes had passed, and I was at my home away from home. Back in the dirt, dust, heat with the smells and death, but I was on the downhill road now. If I could stay alive just a little bit longer, I would see my family once again.

I was back in the saddle once again, finding them and fixing them. Let death rain down on them! From thirty thousand feet, they could not ever hear what killed them. They had dug in; they had turned into moles. Even their hospitals were underground with tunnels everywhere, and I would not have been surprised at all if Vietnam did not cave in and just leave one big hole. Thousands of them must have been buried alive by our big bombs!

Some areas had been classified as free fire zones. Anyone who wanted to could lope some crap into these locations. Artillery, fighter-bombers, B-52's, and even the Battleship *New Jersey,* setting off the coast, could send some in.

One day late in the evening, we were in a free fire zone after a target, when I looked down and saw large craters opening up the ground. *Boy,* I thought, *the artillery must be mad at someone,* but then it dawned on me. We were flying through a B-52 drop. With a quick turn and throttles up, we hauled you know what out of there, praying they would not hit us. It is bad enough to get hit by the Dinks, but to get wiped out by your own ordnance would really be a bad hair day.

The emergency channel was going full blast, and it would have been hard to get a word in on that channel. The weather was rainy, and there were low clouds at Da Nang. Controllers did their very best to get the war planes back in with some shot up, one on fire, and it seemed that all were low on fuel. One would report in saying he had low fuel with only a few minutes of fuel left.

The controller came back, "Roger that, you are number thirteen on the emergency list."

"Well," he replied, "I am going out over the China Sea to punch out. See if you can send a helicopter." I hope they found him.

With our slower aircraft, I had devised a plan that worked for me. I would over-fly the Da Nang beacon and fly east for so many minutes to make sure I would clear the islands, and I would very slowly let down over the water. Usually, there was a clear area consisting of two or three hundred feet between the water and clouds. I would break out and bend it around and head for the beach and pop down on a runway. We always planned to get back with a little reserve fuel, but sometimes our mission would not allow that, and we would be low, much lower than I liked. We could not refuel in air, so we were stuck with what we had. I always considered that having fuel in the tank was like having money in the bank. You could not have enough.

One nice afternoon we had gotten some cooler air in our area. It was a day when you would have enjoyed just being on the river bank fishing, not really caring whether you caught anything, maybe not even putting any bait on the hook, just watching the clouds drift by. The only sound might be the river on its way through time.

Hell, I thought, *maybe a little nap might be in order.* There was no roar of engines and no harsh sounds of explosives to invade and destroy this tranquil setting. I could see this in my mind, but it was not to be.

I had already completed one trip to the badlands that morning and was fixing to head out for another one. I was on the taxiway waiting for take-off instructions from the tower, and I was actually being held for an A-3 on final approach, who had been shot up somewhere up north. On short final, it was observed that he was on fire. He elected to land, and just short of touching down, it must have gotten too hot for him because he punched out. The aircraft hit the runway and bounced into one of the few hangars we had—and blew up. The pilot had enough forward speed to get a full chute, and he landed safely. I just knew that a lot of men worked in that hangar, and this was bad.

I completed my mission and returned to hear that no lives had been lost in the hangar when it went up. It seems that at that time everyone was out in the back for a coffee break. Three "Atta Boys" for the coffee bean.

There was only one major road that ran north and south through the length of Vietnam. There were two lanes at best and sometimes there was only one, and they were made of different materials of whatever happened to be handy at that particular location. The road wove its way up from the south through Da Nang and on north to Hue. Just north of Da Nang, where the mountains meet the sea, was a pass that the road had to go through. Our truck convoys, carrying supplies north to base camps in the Hue area, had to climb up and over this pass before descending into the plain below.

Getting up and over this area was a hellhole deluxe. During my time here, I do not remember a time when traffic moved freely through this area. The high ground that looked down on this pass was ideal for the Dinks who could set up and start having fun with the truck traffic. The Marines did their best with what they had, but the convoys were still ambushed. Vehicles that were disabled were pushed over the side, and what was left continued on. There were a lot of lives lost in this small area. I had worked in this area a lot during my tour there, but I had not seen it from the ground—until this year.

Now, twenty-eight years later, we chugged up the mountains in a sightseeing bus. We stopped at the top, and I really had a good look at ground level. I could envision what it must have looked like to the brave men, who were moving through there not knowing where or when they were going to get hit. The old concrete bunkers and gun mounts are still there, left by the new masters to show the people who travel Route 1 what they had to overcome. The trucks that travel up and over this area now are old. Some that I could identify were made in America and were left behind when we pulled out. There might even be some that were left behind by the French, who had built the concrete bunkers and gun mounts we had observed at the top of the pass. Makes you think a little more about these people and what they can endure.

I often think about the fact that if the roles were reversed, and if an invader was in our country, would we all band together to force them out? These people in Vietnam had fought for centuries to keep out the unwanted. Ho Chi Minh, "Uncle Ho," started as a young man to try to improve his country. He even worked with and for the U.S. Forces in World War II. Someone should have recognized his potential then, and just maybe, he would not have gone north for the help he needed, and we would have a democracy in place there.

Well, back to reality; things were rocking and rolling along. My days were passing by with missions being flown and little battles being fought by brave men under the worst conditions. Jungle warfare is the pits; it had to be like fighting two people with one of the two living with you all the time and trying to bring you down. Body bags were still being delivered and processed in Da Nang, and then flown home to their loved ones.

One morning, shortly before "OK, get up time," they dropped a rocket right at the end of our mess hall. Everyone woke up early that morning. Lucky for us, no one was hurt since the cook and his staff had not yet reported to their duty station. The end of our sleeping quarters took some of the shrapnel. One pilot, who lived at the very end of the building, had his overhead ceiling fan on, which he had had someone send to him. It was cut off, and it dropped on the floor. A locker he had his clothes in was riddled, and so were his clothes, but the young pilot, still in his sack, was untouched. Clean living does pay off.

My replacement was in town, and things were looking up. One thing was still undone. Most units in Nam were someone, and they had a name like "Tigers," "Gunfighter," "Jolly Greens," and so on. We were nothing, just a unit down on the end of the base, and we did our job, even though people did not know what it was.

A few of us got together and decided on a logo. We would be the "Pink Panthers," and overnight that is what we were. Men worked all night painting Pink Panthers on all the aircraft, and even our boss knew nothing of this. Pink Panther badges were made out of beer cans by the locals to pin on our duty uniforms, and still today, I have mine. The Pink Panther stood erect with the cigarette holder, and the sun rose on a Pink Panther world. Everywhere you looked was Mr. Pink Panther. Our boss was delighted and so were we. We were *some*body; we were the Pink Panthers! It is amazing how something like this can uplift morale. "Hey, Dinks, don't mess with us. We are the Pink Panthers!" I hope that this logo still does exist somewhere in our Armed Forces.

I had appointed two new S.I.P.s, who were both gray-hairs. They were not long in the tooth, but long in experience and full of common sense, and they were to be responsible for the check-outs of new pilots coming to the unit. I knew these men would be a credit to the unit and plenty of help to the new pilots, who would need all the help they could get.

Well, it was here. Hopefully, my last trip into the badlands. Out to the trail and further west, hunting was good because there were so many more of their units in the south. Arriving back at the base, it was official. I had orders. I should report to headquarters in Saigon for transportation back to the real world. Good-byes were said.

I was to run across only one of these good men again. Years and years later, at an airport in West Texas, I met my clerk, who kept all of the paperwork, and there was a lot of it. He had gone to flight school under the GI bill, and he was flying a Lear jet for some oil company. He could not tell me much more about his time in Vietnam because he left right after me.

I packed only what I needed; I gave away the rest, and I was on my way. I signed out at headquarters in Saigon and was driven out to the same place I had come in. I was to leave in the morning. The Dinks said good-bye to us at about four o'clock by throwing in a rocket or two. Nothing had changed. Maybe the year had been wasted, but the one thing I knew for sure was a lot of lives had been taken on both sides.

We went back through the same metal building. Only this time, we were on the outgoing side! Our group was subdued, tired, and quiet, and frankly, we just wanted to board and get the hell out of there. I do not believe there was one catcall of, "You'll be sorry." We just looked at them and wondered how many would come back.

9

As soon as the wheels came up, the shouts, which almost hurt your ears, began. We were out of there and going back to the real world, and back to our loved ones. No one could sleep; we were wired up like a Christmas tree. I kept thinking. *Please, please, do not tell me this is a dream!*

Hallelujah. I was back with my family once again. It was so wonderful. They had changed so much and grown inches. I could not get enough of them. My wife, as throughout our Army career, had done a super job of being both mother and father to them. I went through a short period of time being unable to really relax. Plus, I had a few bad dreams that had me out of bed in a flash, but by being with my family and friends each day, I could see improvement. Time goes by now without thinking of it at all.

This year when my wife and I went on a visit back to the same area where I had spent that one year out of my real life, a flood of memories regrouped themselves. The same thing happened to me after the Vietnam Wall in Washington was completed, and I visited it. Standing there viewing the Wall and finding the names of comrades, men whom I had served with, really did something to me. *I could not leave.* I stood in humble silence. When I looked around, I saw hundreds more just like me. This wall is a monument that will help keep alive the memory of those who gave their lives in the service of their country in a war that had no winner. Hopefully, it will help heal the wounds of those who lost loved ones. The division of people on the war in Vietnam will not disappear until all of the lives of those affected have run their cycle.

I was assigned back to the Fourth Army flight detachment, so we would not be uprooted by a move to somewhere else. The children would be able to stay in their same schools and not have to leave their friends. I flew mostly fix-wing type aircraft, but we had helicopters, and I stayed current in both.

The commanding general of the Fourth Army had his headquarters at Fort Sam Houston and used the helicopter frequently. Everyone seemed to dodge this assignment like the plague. When it came my turn in the barrel to fly the General, I really did not know what to expect. What I was to discover was that he had not received any formal training or indoctrination, but he liked to take the controls and fly the machine. Hell, I saw nothing wrong with this. I had an instructor's rating, and over the years had tried to be killed by the best of the worst!

I hopped over to his headquarters and landed on the edge of the parade ground next to the flagpole in front of the building. He came out, and I reported to him with name and rank, and then I beat him to the punch. I asked him if he would like to make the take-off. He did, and that is when things started to go to hell in a handbasket. I should not have parked quite so close to the flagpole, but we salvaged that part and moved into the parade field for departure. By that time, we had all the traffic stopped to watch Dumbo the Clown put on his act. We finally got into the air and went on our merry way. The General was a very fast learner, and after a few more flights, he could handle it like a pro. He seemed to like me, so I started taking him on fix-wing flights to other states under his command. I got to know him fairly well and admired him very much. He was a fine officer, and I hope he is still alive and prospering.

President Johnson decided not to seek another term, mainly because of the war and the emotional disconnection of the country. Not that he had not done many wonderful things in the domestic arena, with Civil Rights and Education at the top of the list—but he opted to return to his beloved ranch in the hill country of Texas. We kept track of him and occasionally supported him with helicopter transportation. As a former President, he was due those honors.

In the meantime, I had noticed that a lot of my fellow pilots had received orders for advanced training, while I was still there in the flight detachment. I called my branch in Washington to receive the cheerful news that once my year stateside was completed, I would be back on my way to Vietnam. Shortage of experienced pilots was the story. It was a blow, but my family and I could cope with it. We were career soldiers taught not to question why, but to do or die, so we would make the best of the time we had remaining together. As a family, time would be spent wisely with not a minute to waste, and we prayed that the good Lord would look after us and protect us. We all know that God moves in mysterious ways. All you have to do is believe in Him. We did——and He made a move on us.

Word gets around from one person to another, and then on to others, and finally they got to me. The words were that the former President's personal pilot was quitting his job, and that the Boss was looking for a replacement. Something about this interested me, so I called a friend in the Secret Service at the ranch to verify it. It was true. The pilot had all these years of kinda being on his own. True, he had certain projects he was responsible for, but these could be completed at his own pace. With the Boss being there all the time with his hands-on supervision from daylight to dark and beyond, it was a little more than what he wanted, so he was bailing out.

I knew that I was not available at this time, but I thought it would be nice to learn about the job and throw my hat in the ring for the future, so I called my friend and got a time he could see me. When I arrived at the ranch, he was in the pool for his morning swim, so our talk took place with him in the nice cool water and me at the edge of the pool with a coat and tie on. The hot sun beamed down, and sweat ran down my neck and back and straight into my boots.

I explained to him that I was not available immediately because I was regular Army and had received a promotion, which carried an obligation to serve for a length of time, and it had not been completed. To this, he replied, "Let's see if I have this right; you have over twenty years of service and cannot get out?"

I went through my spiel once again and explained it once more, and answered his question with a negative.

"Well," he replied, "I will be talking to General (he used a nickname) Wheeler," who was Chairman of the Joint Chiefs of Staff, "tonight, and I will get back to you."

I was then dismissed, and back to town I went. The next day I had a flight to Fort Polk, Louisiana, and upon my return was met by my boss on the ramp at Randolph, Air Force Base. He directed me to do two things in the following order. First, call the former President out at his ranch, and then call Fourth Army headquarters.

I called the President, and he told me that he had talked to General Wheeler, and the General was going to talk to General Westmoreland and hinted that something might be done. With that, he hung up on me.

I then called Fourth Army headquarters, and was told, "Your retirement date is the end of the month. Would you like a few days of leave time?"

Dang, I thought, *in ten days, I would be out of the Army—if I wanted to.*

I talked it over some more with the family, and of course, my better half said, "Whatever you want to do is all right with me. At least we will be together; you will not be halfway around the world!" So the die was cast, and we had no idea how much our lives would be changed in the future.

Libby and I went out to the ranch to meet with the President and to get an idea of what was expected of us. He put us in one of his Lincoln convertibles, along with Congressman Pickle and his wife, and away we went on a tour of the ranch. As we passed his grandfather's house, the Boss remarked that maybe we could live there. Libby had that deer-in-the-headlights look when she heard that.

The house was in a beautiful setting surrounded by live oak trees, which were two hundred years old. It had a view of the river, but the house spoiled this pretty picture. It looked like a strong wind could blow it into the river. It was an ugly color, faded barn red, and believe it or not, the inside of the house was worse. It had not been lived in for quite some time. Paint was peeling off; trash was everywhere; the mice were having a field day, and it would take some doing to make it livable. It was evident that the President wanted us to live there so that we would be close to his house. He gave up on his main selling point when Libby told him that she did not care whose grandfather had lived there; she had a new big house in San Antonio. The nesting instinct in this gal was coming out, big time.

As we walked through the house, the Boss would point out that a little paint here and there would do wonders to make it look like new. The house did have one saving grace, a screened-in front porch, and the President made that his main selling point. He said, "In the summertime, you can move your bed out here. It will be cool and quiet, and only the birds and the sound of the river will be heard." His pitch would have made a used car salesman blush. I felt so sorry for Libby. What a terrible decision she had to make!

David, our son, and I got busy with the painting while Libby and the girls got busy with the cleaning. One day, while Dave and I were painting, the door popped open and there stood the President's cousin. She was dressed in clothes and a flop hat at least three decades out of style. She lived "just up the road apiece," and she wondered what we were doing. We told her that we were painting, and to this she replied, "Oh yes, you are Lyndon's painters."

Poor old soul, even though she was to live another fifteen years, and I was to talk with her quite often, she went to her grave thinking that I was one of Lyndon's painters. The President and Mrs. Johnson had some excellent painters, but I am sorry to say that I was not one of them. I am not sure if Cousin Oreole had a hearing problem because she did all of the talking, but I do know for a fact that she could not see very well. It was a dead give-away when I saw her at the post office in Stonewall reading her mail with a magnifying glass.

This lady also drove an automobile. She ran over irrigation pipes, which we had running all over the ranch, and even a small calf, which could not get out of her way. The President threatened to charge her for all the damage she did, but it was an empty threat because he always looked after her and took care of her. One day in Fredericksburg, her car jumped the curb and hit a store window, breaking out a big display window. She told the store people that she was only paying for half of the window because that was all that fell out.

After the President's cousin had gone to her reward, Mrs. Johnson had Libby go down to her house for a look-see or inventory. One drawer in her nightstand was completely full of eyeglasses that she would buy at the five and dime. All the papers and magazines from years past were stacked under the bed. Endless numbers of empty jars and lids that were used to preserve fruits and vegetables were present. This lady was one of a kind. She must have been very lonely living by herself with her husband gone, and with no family but her cousin, who always invited her to every event that took place at the ranch.

At last we were finally moved. The nice big house in San Antonio had been sold, and we were settling into our new home in the Texas hill country. With only two bedrooms, the girls had to bunk together. Our son was off in college, and when he came home, he flopped on the couch. We did not see that much of him, but now and then, he would drop in with a big bag of dirty clothes that he knew his mother wanted to do for him. I did notice that he liked to get his feet under his mother's table for a good home-cooked meal. The girls were in their new schools and on their way to making new friends, whom they still see some thirty years later. We were a family unit once again.

In all fairness, I will say that in taking my new job, I was told that flying would be only part of my duties, and I would learn all phases of the ranching operation. In fact, I was looking forward to this after spending what seemed like half of my life in the air. This country boy, having been away so long, was going back to the country. It would be fun and it was.

I had a list of the duties that I would perform in the daily operation of the ranch. A few of these duties were being a purchasing agent and pickup agent for equipment and supplies used at the ranch. I was responsible for the well-being and security of all wild life. Each pasture was fenced to make them deer proof, and we had an abundant deer and turkey population. Plus, we had exotic wild animals from different countries in the world.

I would learn the principles of irrigation, then observe, and improve upon them. Hell, during the dry season, we had two or three pumps going day and night pulling water from the river and pushing it to remote areas of the ranch. I was to schedule preventive maintenance on all equipment. I was in charge of all the fuel that was used in the operation of the ranch, and the good Lord knows, we had fuel tanks everywhere. I am not sure that I ever found them all. I had other duties also, but my mind has since blocked them out. Down at the bottom of this list of duties (it was almost like an afterthought), I was to fly the King Air airplane and the Jet Ranger helicopter.

I was getting my feet on the ground, and my prior tenure was to help me very much. I had flown so much in this area, and I pretty well knew where everything was. I probably knew as much, if not more, about the outlying ranches than most of the other people involved in the operation. I had a ranch pickup truck to get around in, which was radio equipped and not the kind you listen to music on. When the Boss wanted to get ahold of you, it was now—and not a little bit later. Everyone had a radio. They even installed one in the house where we lived, and I suspect that Libby turned it off during the daytime because it seemed like the signal boys were always coming down to check it out.

It was really a phobia with the Boss; if he got on the radio, and he did not get an answer, questions were asked. "Was your radio malfunctioning? Were you out of your vehicle? Where in the hell were you? I needed to talk to you!"

This did not happen very often, but when it did, the sky suddenly turned black and then fell on your head. I understood what he hoped to achieve with this hands-on thing, but just coming from a life or death situation, I completely failed to understand the importance of getting someone on the radio.

No one escaped this man who owned the airways, not even Mrs. Johnson, who was always on her way home from Austin in the early evening. The call would be heard by all. "Bird, where are you?"

The answer would nearly always be the same. "Just coming through Dripping Springs, Darling." This always fascinated me to no end. How in the hell did he know to call her just when she was coming through this area?

In some ways, it was hard to understand what this man expected of you. He had just returned from running our country during wartime to take charge of the ranch and his office. As a former President this was extensive, but it did not bind him to duties. All of the energy that he had used to lead and direct this nation was now focused on one county in Texas. The angels withdrew, and we received the full brunt of the result.

The secretarial staff would be in tears, and the rest of us would be walking around with the seat of our britches flapping in the breeze. This bothered most of those who had contact with him, but not me. To me, this was great. The Dinks did not fire any rockets into grandfather's house. No one shot the windscreen out of my truck. No 37 mm came at me while I was flying. I was in high cotton.

He had told me, when I first came out there, that he did not have to be at any special place at any special time, so he said, "If you think that the weather is bad, we will not go." I will always remember that.

There have been those who have put pressure on their pilots and had a big hand in making them exceed the limitations of themselves and their aircraft, and now these people are lying side by side in the graveyard. Not once did this happen to me, and I will always be thankful. In all honesty, I hope that if I had been put in that position, I would have told them what they could do with the job. My life and the lives of my passengers are too precious to do something stupid and end everything known to us on Earth. It was so reassuring to know that I would never be put in that position.

It was the period of hard work and long hours with being up before sunrise and praying that the sun would soon sink away. There were always fun times that would make it all worthwhile. It had been a long summer, but now it was behind us. The hay had been baled and stored. The cattle on all the ranches had been worked; the fields had been plowed to receive the oats for winter grazing, and things were slowing down, so the Boss told me to take some days off.

Fine with us. We had never been to Carlsbad Caverns, and we thought it would be nice to visit there. The day before we were to leave on our trip, I was in the headquarters area when the Boss stopped me and asked me when we were leaving. I told him, and he reached into his pocket and pulled out a roll of paper money. They appeared to all be one hundred dollar bills.

"Here," he said, "buy your sweet wife a dress and get your daughters something." He kept on with his, "Do this and do that," and all the time he was handing me one hundred dollar bills. "Have a good time and come back when you're tired of doing nothing."

I was amazed to see this part of this man, but in the years to come, I would witness many more things, like and unlike this incident, that would give me an insight to this man that few people other than family would ever have.

Our insurance company required me to have a factory-checkout in both the King Air airplane and the Jet Ranger helicopter, so I got that out of the way by going to Wichita, Kansas, to the Beechcraft factory for the King Air and to the Bell factory, located near Arlington, Texas, for the Jet Ranger. Both of these machines were turbine powered. I was legal now and flew each one enough to keep my hand in, but my ranch duties occupied the bulk of my daylight time. I might fly the President into Austin in the morning, just to turn around and come back to put on my ranch hat. Maybe in the evening, I would go pick him up, or he would drive back. I was plenty busy, but enjoying every bit of it.

In the fall of that first year, the Boss decided that we had too many deer in the home pastures, so we went about setting up a way to capture them and transport them to the outlying ranches. We contacted the state wildlife people and received information on how to catch them. We borrowed a net from the county game warden, and we were in business.

What it amounted to was putting some poles so far apart to hang the net on and a tree had to be in the vicinity of the trap. Two or three nights before we were ready to catch the deer, we would bait them with corn under the net. When we observed that we were getting the deer coming to the corn, we would set our trap. By pushing a device, it would cause a small explosive charge to detonate, and the effect was the release of the net. That was my job.

About one hour before darkness, I would bait the trap and retire to the tree and wait. I could not make a sound, and I could not move a muscle. This would have been excellent training for a sniper. I had a hand radio with me, but I had to keep it shut off until the last minute. Since we had so much traffic on it, the deer would have left the country.

When I had ten to fifteen deer under the drop, I would drop the net on them, turn on the radio, call out that the net was down, and the troops waiting just over the hill would get high behind to my location. They brought with them a boxed-in trailer to put captives in. They would arrive, and the rodeo would start. It was not easy to get a bunch of deer, who were tangled up in the net, loose without hurting them or you. They could hurt you with their horns, and their hooves were razor sharp. Believe me, they were trying to get away. We would finally prevail, and we would have them in the trailer, and on their way to a new home.

We moved hundreds of them, and really did not lose very many. Now and then, when we off-loaded at the new location, there might be one or two who did not make it. I would guess that these deer had hurt themselves trying to escape the trailer, and their heart had failed them. By the time we had transferred enough of them, I had spent so much time in a tree that I was beginning to think and act like an owl.

The President would be proved right on his decision to move and thin out the deer population. The next year we could see that the deer were doing much better, and the year after that, we could really see the results. They were much bigger; the horns were much improved, and the survival rate during the winter was up. It does help to give Mother Nature a hand now and then.

The exotics needed even more help. The black buck antelopes were from India and could not stand cold weather. I remember one extremely cold winter, which is unusual for this area, with snow and ice all around. We lost black bucks by the hundreds from hypothermia, but then at the same time, the zoo in Dallas lost animals also. It was a bad time everywhere.

What happens to animals with hypothermia is that each day, if this condition continues, they lose a portion of their body heat, and they slowly freeze to death. I would find them under a tree, lying in a normal resting position––it was their eternal resting position, as they had literally froze to death.

We tried to combat this in different ways. We'd start our feeding program early in the fall with high protein feeds to put a layer of fat on their bodies. Then every day during the winter, we would feed a high protein supplement at the same time and at the same site whether it was rain, shine, or ice. In this way, we hoped to get the maximum number of deer to feed. We would still lose a few, but we had cut our losses. Now all these years later, I believe that the new generations have developed a tolerance to these conditions. Isn't Mother Nature something?

In one pasture, we had a lot of exotics and in this particular pasture, the oat field was deer-proof fenced. Now, the fields were determined by being level with better soil and fewer rocks, and this one worked out just right. Between the outer fence and the oat field, the distance was only about fifty yards. It was an ideal place to direct the exotics into and catch their little butts. The Boss wanted me involved in this with the chopper.

Now with your mind as open as you can get it at this time, visualize this. Forty grown men from all walks of life were in a line going through this pasture, and I was in a helicopter trying to push these animals into the bottleneck and trap them. Now, some of these people were Secret Service agents; some were White House signal people; some were ranch hands, and some were people the Boss commandeered on the way to the pasture. If video had been available then, as it is now, someone would have had a best seller. We'd make a catch and move them to new homes. This was kind of a one-time deal. We could not hope to get all this manpower back again, so it was back to the owl in the tree thing again.

Now, let it be known that in one pasture, we had an English red stag, who was as big as a horse and meaner than a rattlesnake. He had even attacked a tractor on the way to the oat field, and praise the Lord, one night he fell under our net. One of the Secret Service agents was helping out, and in the subduing, he was kicked in the wrist, and he broke his watch.

The Boss, who was right in there with us, hollered, "Don't worry about that. I'll get you another."

So we had the king of the hill in our power. We sawed his horns off and relocated him. I saw him later, and he was as mean as he had been before.

I have failed to mention another type of animal we had at the ranch. A Cambodian antelope, called a Nelgi, was almost as tall as a small horse. The male was a dark color and from a distance, with the sun shining on him, would have a bluish tint. The female was a tan color and did not grow to be as large as the male. The one thing that they had in common was that they were both funny looking. From the front, they sloped down to the rear quarters. No straight back line here. It would appear, by looking at them, that they would be awkward. Far from it. They could really cover the ground. In one pasture, it appeared that we were overstocked with these animals, and the Boss decided to sell some of them.

The Oklahoma City Zoo wanted some, so a deal was struck. We had a trap at the end of the pasture that had a high fence on three sides, so we got busy and figured out a way to close off the trap once I ran them in with the helicopter. We were set. The zoo boys were there to receive the animals. Gathering the animals with the helicopter worked pretty well with most animals. I would take it slow and easy. I would try to work them into a tight little group and take them down a fence line, which helped to hold them together.

These creatures, which Mrs. Johnson referred to as God's mistake, would turn back under me, and I would be forced to go back and start the drill all over again. It must have taken an hour to get enough of them into the trap, and these animals had been running most of the time. When I saw that they were trapped, I flew back to headquarters, and then returned to the trap site in my truck.

I was not prepared for what I saw. Most of the Nelgi were down. The zoo boys had shot them with a tranquilizer gun, and ten of them were dead. I am sure that they had figured the weight of the animals correctly, but they had not realized how hot these animals had gotten in the time it took me to get them into the trap. It was a sad sight. If they had not been in such a hurry to load out, it would have been different. The Boss asked the head zoo man if he wanted some more brought into the trap. He shook his head in the negative. At five hundred dollars a pop, he had all of a good thing he could stand. I felt sorry for him with the long drive back to Oklahoma. He was empty handed, and he had to explain to his boss what had happened.

We utilized the helicopter in a number of ways. I would fly the Boss to Austin and land on the roof of the Federal Building. He would walk down a flight of steps and enter an elevator that would take him to his office. The time frame from the ranch to the office was about the same whether we used the *King Air* or the helicopter. After his library was completed, a pad was put on the roof for the same purpose.

It was also used to visit and inspect outlying ranches, and it was especially handy to check water gaps after a really hard rain. It could take two days for men on horseback to do what I could do in thirty minutes. Plus, I could then direct a repair team to just the ones that needed to be replaced. It was as handy as a slice of bread.

One day, during the dry season, we had two, maybe three pumps, working day and night, pulling the water out of the river and pushing it onto our thirsty crops and grasses. The river flow showed a measurable decrease. Our pumps would soon be sucking sand. The Boss had at one time told me that the water that goes over the dam is lost forever. Maybe he just said that to inspire us to keep the pumps going or just maybe because he had the two dams put in, he thought it was his water. I will never know.

One weekend when all the President's family was present (and they did get together quite often), the Boss instructed me to take his only grandson in the helicopter to go chase the deer. This two-and-a-half-year-old boy, full of piss and vinegar, son of the President's youngest daughter, thoroughly enjoyed this. This was the start of a relationship that is still on-going.

As he grew older, an inquisitive mind brought forth the endless questions. "What is that? What does it do? How much does it cost?"

I do not know where he got that last one. As we both grew older, he would fly with me a lot. At first I sat him on a pile of books, so he could see out of the cockpit, and I was all the time threatening to beat his little butt if he did not leave the controls alone.

Then the time came, when like overnight, he grew up. I could throw the set of books away, and now he had to adjust the seat and rudder pedals to the lower and outward position. Time does fly when you are having fun. I had gone bird hunting with him and his dad when the shotgun he used was taller than he was, but now he had grown up. He could land the airplane himself with me lightly handling the controls. Then the time came when I could sit back, with my arms folded, as he would grease in a landing.

I had always been against anyone born with the proverbial silver spoon in their mouth, probably because deep down in my subconscious that had not happened to me. I had seen so many people who were born with all of the advantages not amount to a hill of beans, and they did not make a single contribution to society. This young man, who grew up almost totally surrounded by females, has proven me wrong. Accepting an R.O.T.C. commission from the University, he served overseas, became jump qualified, and attended flight school. Now, after completing his service to his country, he has completed law school and has been admitted to the bar. I have fun with this one, berating him for not picking out an honorable profession. I may be fooling myself, but I like to think that, just maybe, I had a little bit of a part in this.

I do not know if with the kids in school, Libby got bored, or just let herself get conned into it, or what, but anyhow, she was working as a volunteer for the Johnson Foundation at the birthplace of President Johnson. No big deal for her, as it was only about three hundred yards from the grandfather's house, so she would just walk down there, and show visitors through the birthplace. She enjoyed it. It was not hard work and she, unlike me, has a way with people.

One night, when I got home, she had a story to tell me. She had been cleaning house when a Secret Service agent came to our door and informed her that the President wanted her down at the birthplace. She reported there, and the President introduced her to the Secretary of Interior and to some other people, including the Director of National Parks. It seems that the Boss was giving them some land, which included his birthplace and his boyhood home in Johnson City. The President told these people that he wanted these women, who had been helping as volunteers, to represent him in the houses.

What she wanted to tell me, and she did, was that she did not know for sure, but she thought she might be working for the government. She was and did work for the government for over twenty-four years and ended up the last ten years as the curator of the L.B.J. National Historic Site. I think that she really enjoyed what she was doing, especially in the later years after our family members had left home and had families of their own. I do know she had a lot of fun running around the country, spending someone else's money to furnish the Johnson Settlement cabin and the boyhood home. President Johnson was always bringing people down to show them where he was born, and he would always introduce Libby to them. She was always meeting famous and infamous people.

We, the ranch hands, would meet at six A.M. in the kitchen of the ranch house; coffee would be ready, and we would plan out what we would do that day. Our Boss was present, so it was short and sweet. No wasted time was spent on shop talk.

We would usually move and reset the pipe that we had set just before sunset the night before. We all had rubber boots, and the Boss had gotten himself a pair, so we all moved out to move the pipe. We were a little bit faster without the Boss helping us, but he was there, and he would grab one end of the pipe and help us complete the move. I had nightmares about him climbing over a ten-foot high, deer-proof fence, but he made it over all of them.

With the pipe reset, we would move on to other duties. The Boss would return to the ranch house, have some breakfast, and jump back into bed. I think it was a game that he enjoyed playing, but just before lunchtime, here he was again trying to push us on through the lunch hour. As the sun was sinking out of sight, he would magically appear with a task that just had to be completed right now, so into the darkness we went. He was not a slave-driving boss in any sense of the word, but he truly loved this little game he played with us.

One really hot day, I was baling hay, and doing my dead level best to complete the field before dark, when here he was again. He had gone by the grandfather's house and picked up Libby and had one or two others with him.

"Shut it down and go with us," he shouted.

"Well, I had planned to finish this field before dark," I said.

"It will wait until tomorrow. It isn't going to rain tonight, so come on, we are going to town to eat dinner."

"Run me by the house so I can clean up a little," I replied.

"You can wash up in town."

So there I sat down to a steak dinner, looking like a sharecropper, covered with dirt and grease with the former President of the United States. It did not bother him one little bit—so I figured, what the hell, it would not bother me.

Another time, along these same lines, I was flying my Boss and some others into Austin for a dinner party. Libby had been invited, and on the way in, he asked her if a little country girl from Richland Springs, Texas, had ever thought she would be flying into Austin to have dinner. Her reply was no, that she had not even dreamed of it.

To this, he replied, "This little old boy from Johnson City never thought he would be doing this either." He quickly added for Libby's benefit, "Get ready for a rough landing in Austin. He always bounces me around."

Immediately coming to my defense, Libby replied, "He will not!"

Not knowing what had been insinuated about my flying ability, I was not unlike the old blind cow that found the acorns. It was a landing that does not happen every time. It was one where everything works out just right, and you do not even know you are on the runway. As a matter of fact, it was so smooth you still had a sensation of flying.

The Boss countered with, "Well, that was just because you were aboard. He always bounces me."

He loved to tease, sometimes in a gruff manner, which could irritate some people, but once you got to know him, you would see right through it.

It was either the first or second Christmas that we spent at the ranch that this event took place. A convoy of brand-new Ford Sedan vehicles arrived at the ranch headquarters. All were exactly alike with the exception of color. Word was passed by the staff that they were for the ranch hands, and they were invited to pick out the color that they liked and put their name on that particular vehicle. My name was not on the list, even though

I considered myself one of them. I blew it off. Hell, I had wheels and a pickup suited my needs just fine. Before I could give it anymore thought, the Boss informed me that the reason my name was not on the list was that I could use any of his vehicles that he was not using at that very moment. This led to the fact that from then on forward until his death, and a period after that, until someone figured it out, I still was driving the President's Lincoln Continentals.

Starting from the time frame, when the Boss got out of office, Henry Ford number two, would send their top of the line Ford, the Mark, to the ranch each year. Upon receiving this car, the Boss would drive it once or twice, complaining all the time that there was no headroom. He could not wear his hat while he was driving, and he wanted to do so. One year we even tried to lower the seat rails, but that did not work, so being short in stature paid off. I drove it so much that the folks in Fredericksburg thought I was the Mark dealer because I had a new one every year.

What a Christmas that was for us, the ranch hands. At the last minute, the Boss wanted me to fly his oldest daughter and her husband to Acapulco for a second honeymoon, and his instructions were to take my better half and his head Secret Service agent and wife, plus a Spanish-speaking agent. His parting words were, "Have a good time. It's on me."

On the way down, the Spanish speaker informed us that he really knew a good place to get a steak at a good price. We went blindly along with him to this best of dining deals. The tip-off should have been when we were seated on the sidewalk. I do not remember if the food was of any account, but I do know that it is hard to enjoy anything when you eat with one hand and have to use the other hand to fight the flies off your food.

While there, we received a call from the ranch to tell us that our oldest daughter had been in an accident but was fine except for some bumps and bruises. What had happened from the information we received was that while at the Christmas party at the hangar, our Sandy had to go home to the grandfather's house for a female thing. The falling freezing rain made the roadway slick and en route she left the roadway and cut down a power pole. Bystanders who saw what had happened, told us later that they had no idea how our Sandy got out of the truck without being turned into a crispy critter. Thank the Lord she did.

When we got back home, I was to find out that when our Sandy found out she had to go home, she jumped into the first ranch vehicle she came to, which happened to be a brand new pickup with just a few miles on it. In fact, it had just been driven out from Austin, and this pitiful piece of iron was in the shape of a horseshoe. I knew I was going to hear about this.

A few days later, the Boss said, "Let's go for a ride."

This is it, ran through my mind. *Get braced. Here comes the bull with the big horns.*

We went riding in the pasture in one of his four-door convertibles, and when we were out aways, he said, "Don't be too hard on Sandy and let me tell you why. When I was young, my father got a brand new Ford, and I wrecked it. But to show his faith in me, he went and got another one and had me drive it all around Johnson City to show everyone I was still driving." I learned a great big lesson from that one.

This was the very same daughter, who from the time she could talk, would always reply that she wanted a horse anytime someone would ask what she would like for some special occasion. How in the world could we do this? We were always in a foreign country or in quarters on post, but the move to the L.B.J. Ranch afforded that opportunity.

We asked the Boss if we might pasture a horse in the river bottom below our house, and he agreed, so our daughter soon had her very own horse. No more sweat walking horses for hours at Fort Sam Houston just to be able to ride for a few minutes. Sandy had her own live horse, so to speak, in her own front yard, and she was in hog heaven. She lived with that hobo horse and rode it all the time.

One day in riding around the ranch, she observed that some cattle had gotten into a field of hay where they were not supposed to be, so she lit into getting them out. Just when she almost had gotten them back out, the Boss arrived and sounded off the bullhorn he had on his car. This scattered the cows like a flushed covey of quail. The agent in charge, who was with the Boss at this time, told this to me. Sandy had dismounted from her horse to tighten the cinch to her saddle, when the Boss came rolling in yelling at Sandy to get mounted and get around the cows and get them out of the field. This noisy arrival spooked her horse, and he jerked loose from her.

His next words were, "Sandy, hurry up and catch your horse and get those damn cows out of there."

They would have been out of there already, if the Boss would have known how to react to animals, but he did not. What I was told, happened next was, this petite blonde looked him straight in the eye and said, "You go to hell."

With that she went to catch her horse and went on home to tell her mother that she had gotten Daddy fired. I doubt if anyone ever said that to him before or afterwards, and he never did say anything to me about it. He was man enough to keep it between Sandy and himself, and his attitude toward her did not change. Just maybe, he admired her for standing up to him.

Nearly everyone told him what they thought he wanted to hear, rather than saying, "Hell no––that's not right!" As a matter of fact, a short time later, the Boss appeared at a picnic that Sandy's Spanish class was having down by the river, so I am sure that he did not retain any bad feelings toward our daughter.

We had a gate left open to one of our deer pastures. Of course, one of the English red stags found it and promptly seized the opportunity and freed himself. We tried in vain to haze him back in, but he was enjoying his newfound freedom far too much to fall for this. The Boss had me go get the chopper and try my luck. I fell back on my old tactic of bringing him down the fence line, but just as I would get him almost to the opening, he would double back underneath me, and I would have to start over again.

I have failed to tell you that we had a blocking agent in place consisting of people on foot and in vehicles. One of these was the Boss in one of his four-door ragtop Lincolns. After about four attempts, in which the stag turned under me, I had almost gotten him to the gate, when I observed the Boss step out of his car and pull his saddle gun from the rack under the seat. He brought it to his shoulder, and I was looking directly at the wrong end of the barrel.

Good Lord, I had survived Vietnam and now I was going to be shot down on the L.B.J. Ranch! But to my surprise and relief, the animal dropped dead in his tracks. This event occurred from a distance of better than seventy-five yards and better yet, it happened looking through eyeglasses almost one quarter of an inch thick. This man never ceased to amaze me.

He later told me that we were using up too much time, and he decided to put an end to it. Maybe he wanted to show off another one of his many skills.

About one year after I had started my new job, I was given a mission by my Boss. Two Mexican nationals, who had work permits and with whom I had worked on the Ranch, returned to Mexico to tie up loose ends and ready their families for a move. I was told to go get them and process them out of Mexico for entry into this country. The legal part of this had been completed. I flew to Guadalajara, Mexico, and picked up one of the families—and then I went back to Monterrey, where the other family met us at our consulate. They all had to have physicals and much paperwork was filled out.

Finally, this was completed and out to the airport we went. A problem arose after filing the flight plan. They looked at the flight plan and looked at our airplane, and then they figured out that I had more souls on board than I had passenger seats. I explained that the little ones would be tied in on the laps of their parents. For a while, it looked like a no-go, but after a few American dollars were passed around, we were in the air, bound for the L.B.J. Ranch. My orders from the Boss were to call him about twenty minutes out with my ETA for the ranch because he wanted to meet the airplane.

I could hear all the talk that was taking place on our radio commo. The White House Signal boys called the Boss and told him that President Nixon wanted to talk to him.

His reply was, "Tell him that I am out in the pasture, and you cannot get me."

A few minutes later there was another call to the Boss. "Sir, they said they are holding Air Force One on the ground in Tyler, Texas, and they really need to talk to you."

The reply was the same as before and followed by, "He is trying to get me. I am not trying to get him."

Upon landing, there he was with bags of jelly beans for each child. For years, the little ones referred to him as the "jelly-bean man." Those children, who were of age, were soon in the Head Start School just across the river from the ranch.

The Boss had given me money prior to the trip to pay for all of this. I had kept a detailed account of all the money I spent, including the bribe to the airport officials at Monterrey. The next day he found me out on the ranch and asked me if the money had been adequate. I gave him my written account, which came to fifty cents more than he had given me. He reached into his pocket, even though I was saying, "Forget it."

He did not have a fifty-cent piece, so he turned to his SS agent for it while saying, "I knew not to give you too much money as you would not have come back." He knew how to have fun with a person while planting a seed of doubt in your mind.

One of these men, whom I had processed into the country, went to work for the park system after the President's death. He was a hard-working family man, who retired a few years ago, and whom we laid to rest last winter. I will miss him.

There were long hours and hard work, but there were also fun times and lots of perks. We would be invited down to the Big House every so often for dinner and that was always fun. The first time our youngest daughter went with us for one of these dinners, I am sure was a big experience for her. She was seated next to the Boss, and he gave her his full attention.

What she was not prepared for were his eating habits. He would lift his dessert plate to his chin and scoop the food into his mouth until it was all gone. Peggy Ann did well, and we were proud of her. Her eyes got a little bit bigger, but that was the only indication from her during this procedure.

Former Prime Minister Wilson from England came to the ranch for a visit with the Boss, and one afternoon they decided to play golf at the local course in Fredericksburg, and I was to fly them there in our helicopter. We arrived at the first hole and after a couple of practice drives, one thing was very obvious.

Mr. Wilson had played this game before and was on top of it. They teed off and right away things started to turn sour for the Boss. The further we went, the worse things got. The Boss resorted to hitting two balls, and taking the one which gave him the best advantage. That did not help. He was getting his pants beat off by the Prime Minister. When the Boss could not stand anymore of this drubbing, he told the Prime Minister we would have to leave and return to the ranch because his pilot had to get back and sell rodeo tickets.

The Prime Minister shot a glance at me, and I nodded my head in the affirmative. We flew back to the ranch and to this day, I am quite sure there was not a rodeo going on within a hundred miles of us. I figure that if you can't be loyal to your boss, chances are, you would not be loyal to your spouse or to yourself.

Summer was back with us. The hot sun beamed down on us and sucked the moisture out of the land, and to some degree out of the bones of those of us who were in the fields setting or moving the irrigation pipe. I must have been doing a good job of ranching because I began to notice that the Boss would call in the military, which he had access to as a former President, to fly him here and there. We moved pipes in mud so thick that it would suck your rubber boots off if you were not careful. Sweat ran the full length of your backbone, and this scene was broken up by the sound of a military aircraft up in the cool air taking my Boss to town.

The Boss, with his reluctance to pull me off my ranch duties to fly him, had sent my morale into a nose-dive. This went on for a period of time, and finally I talked to him about it. I told him that I was not getting enough flying time to stay proficient on the machines, and he agreed with me and allowed that he would correct the problem. Within a very short time frame, he made good on his word. We had a deal with A.M.P.I. (Associated Milk Producers, Inc.) headquartered in San Antonio. I was to fly a minimum of forty hours a month for them with the stipulation that whenever the Boss needed me to fly for him that would take precedence, and they would go another way.

Things changed in a heartbeat, and this was one of them. We were to move so that the new ranch foremen could move into the grandfather's house. We consulted with the Boss on where we might move. In our deal, the airplane was to be based at the ranch, so our home needed to be close. His reply to us was like this, "Well, I should recommend Johnson City as it was my boyhood home, but the German people in Fredericksburg have character, and I think it would be a nice place for y'all to live and raise your family."

We found a lovely old house in Fredericksburg, bought it, and moved in, and I am sure it will be our final home. It was different, but it was great.

I would contact the general manager's secretary every week to receive my trips for the next week. I would be told where to be and at what time, and where they were to be taken. I'm talking about the people, who were on the payroll of AMPI. This company was in the act of expansion and putting together small milk cooperatives into a giant unit that could control the price of milk products.

I had stepped into something new, and it was fun. I would pick up people in the northern states, and we would go to other places in other states, and the personnel that I had picked up would be talking to dairy farmers and trying to convince them that the right path to receiving the best price for their milk was to be an entity of AMPI. It really was.

As a big unit, they had a bigger say in what would happen to them as to selling their milk, and what price they would receive for the product. By banding together, they had control of their product, and the price they would receive. What could be better? Like safety in numbers, things could only get better. This endeavor was the best thing that could happen to them.

Being a member of the nation's largest dairy association had numerous advantages, with the best being a Washington lobby to help increase the price support of their product. I would like to say up front, and before I forget it, these people, who were members, directors, and management, were the salt of the Earth. They were hard working, God-fearing, dairymen, who believed the old-fashioned way about God and country and the right to produce a product for a fair price. I was to become friends with many of these people and was to visit their farms.

During this time frame, there were more of these small individual units, unlike now, with big operators milking thousands of cows around the clock. These dairy farms had been handed down to the next generation. Now one thing that these old country boys learned really fast was that cream comes to the top, and they figured out a way to get their share.

When Richard Nixon became President, they realized they had backed the wrong candidate, but they got busy to correct this problem. They knew how to get hold of the cream when it came to the top, but they were not real sharp people in how they put their political money to work. In fact, the people who put this giant unit together could not run it. They were outstanding organizers, but they could not operate the unit after they put it together. Their use of political money was to do them in. As a matter of fact, two of them ended up spending time in a federal country club for their part in this action. This consisted of secret cash donations and laundered corporate funds. This was compounded by destroying court-ordered documents about the transactions.

I did remember flying a man around the country, who carried only a briefcase and made short stops at various places. These people were never to work at AMPI again. After the new management got their ducks lined up and the federal civil-antitrust suit was in the process of being put behind them, they got down to doing what they knew best and that was producing milk products. They would end up controlling the bulk of milk products in the country, most of which is produced in the central part of our country.

I had a lot of fun going through the plants that processed cheese, ice cream, and other products made from milk. I do not understand why, but cows produce more milk in the spring. This surplus would be turned into powder. This dry powder was easily stored and could easily be restored into fluid milk by adding water. A lot of this was shipped to other countries, which were in need of wholesome food.

Shortly before Christmas each year, they would send me up north to pick up a load of cheese. It would be processed in small packages with all the different varieties they made in their plants. It would be given to employees and friends as Christmas presents. Also at this time of the year, President Johnson would send me to Dallas to pick up a load of toys for both boys and girls to be given to the little ones. I got to thinking that maybe I was a flying Santa Claus.

I really was enjoying this new setup. Whenever the President would want me to take him somewhere, I would notify the milk boys, and they would make other arrangements. I was getting a lot of flying time and having a ball. Each month the Boss would send me down to San Antonio to settle up with the milk producers. In our deal, they would pay my "away from home" money. They would cut two checks, one for me and one for the company. Mine was the smaller of the two.

The milk people were more than good to me. They treated me like one of their own. I was never left to cool my heels at the airport. I even attended a lot of meetings; in fact, so many that I would be asked where my dairy was located. I knew most of the directors as I would pick them up around the country and bring them to a central location for their get-togethers. I could leave the ranch before the sun ever thought about coming up and make a trip to the northern states, attend a late night meeting, and return to the ranch about twenty-four hours later.

As I would taxi to the hangar, which was close to the main house, the Boss would hit me on our L.B.J. radio and ask me where I had been. Then he would tell me that he was the only person awake when I left and when I returned. Then he would go on to say, "Nobody else gives a damn about you. What are you going to do when I am gone? God Bless."

Sometimes he could really be full of it, but it was nice to know that someone was thinking of me after a long hard trip. The truth being known, I probably woke him up coming and going with a noisy airplane.

It was really enjoyable flying the Boss around, as he would always introduce me to his friends. I have gotten to meet a lot of notable people this way. Our N number in the airplane was N601T, which had been on the previous aircraft owned by the Boss. Air controllers around the state knew the aircraft number and would give us special treatment. When I filed the flight plan, I would put Code 1 in the remarks section, which was afforded to presidents or former presidents. In the State of Texas, controllers would hold up air carriers to get us off or on the ground. Even when I did not file, they would ask if the Boss was aboard. My negative answer would turn me into a sharecropper again.

In a valley, really in the middle of nowhere, nested neatly with mountains on two sides was this Hacienda. It was like something you would see in a Hollywood production. It had a big courtyard with flowing fountains, a swimming pool, and an area to play tennis. It was neat and nice. It was quiet at night, off the air routes, where the sound of aircraft could not reach your ears. The only sound was the cry of a coyote, maybe calling for his mate, who had not yet returned to their temporary home. It was the ideal place for me. Vietnam was still on my mind, and this was so soothing. No one was trying to do me in, and there were no duties to perform once I had flown the Boss into his getaway/hideaway.

It was an arid land with very little rainfall most of the time, and it was a landscape stunted by dryness that appeared miniature in comparison with the large oak trees that we were blessed with in our part of Texas. This ranch, which surrounded the Hacienda, consisted of over one hundred thousand acres, and it lay about one hundred air miles south, southeast of Chihuahua City. It was close to nothing. You had a two-hour drive by land, interrupted by umpteen gates and bad roads, and you would arrive at a town, where you might get products and services that you needed. Needless to say, most of what was needed was flown in.

In the aviation department, we were in hog heaven. We had a long, hardstand runway and a large metal hangar that would hold two DC-3's. Former President Miguel Aleman then owned the ranch. It was said that the former President was only on the ranch twice in his lifetime––once when construction on the Hacienda was started and once again with his wife when it was completed. She did not like it, so they did not return. Her loss, my gain. I really loved it; I would have sold my soul to have a ranch like this.

It worked like this; the Boss and an old lifetime friend made up two of the three partners, and the third was a Mexican national, who headed up the tourist department of Mexico. I think that he was close to both the former President of Mexico and my Boss. President Aleman had visited the L.B.J. Ranch before. The ranch that I saw through my eyes was lovely in a harsh way. It took a lot of land to keep a cow going, but hell, there was a lot of land there.

The Boss always wanted to improve conditions, so one of the first actions was to pull in all the cattle for a health check. I flew our vet down to the ranch to personally inspect and correct health problems. Cows were culled for age and other reasons. The Boss was deadly serious about improving his herd. To further show he meant what he wanted, we were to gather about fifty of our best two-year-old purebred Hereford bulls from the L.B.J. Ranch in Texas and turn them loose on this ranch in Mexico. The bulls had fun for a while. We know that for a fact because the next year we could see the evidence of this.

We had told the ranch foreman to pull the bulls out of the pastures after sixty days and put them back on a feeding program. The ranch foreman was a sergeant in the Mexican Army and had a radio link to Mexico City. Well, he did not carry out this task of pulling the bulls out and putting them on feed. Our pampered bulls went to hell in a handcart in very short order. Those that we did find were a walking bag of bones and hide. It had been too large of a transition for them to make. Heat, insects, and having to cover ten miles to fill one of his stomachs, had diminished his sex life, and had put him into the survival mode, and after a while that too went away. Then the next year we would judge the results, and I would say that we had made some improvement and maybe in some way we got our seed back.

The ranch was divided into eight and ten thousand acres fenced in pastures with one family living on it. "Living" may be too strong of a term to use. A hut in the middle of the pasture was their home, and all the cattle were their responsibility. They lived in a house where you could throw a cat through any wall, and they had pigs on the stoop with the young children playing with the pigs. It could be compared with places I had seen in Vietnam.

Generations had grown up here and had never been off the ranch. The Boss wanted very much to do something about the horrid conditions which existed on this ranch. Little ones learned from their parents, who in turn learned from their parents. Not much of a chance existed for anything new to be added to this system. What they really learned was the art of survival. They were cut off from the real world. Their world was the pasture and cows, with the hut in the middle of it.

The Boss jumped on this condition with both feet. A teacher was hired; a building was designated the schoolhouse, and most likely the first Head Start in Mexico was on its way. Clothes of all sizes for male and female and medical supplies of all kinds were rounded up back in Texas and transported down to L.B.J. South. The Boss even sent down some of his fancy shirts with French cuffs and pleated frills. I am pretty sure that he had worn some of these shirts at State dinners and other formal occasions.

It so happened that there was only one cowboy who was the exact size of the President, so he received the shirts. Now, picture this if you can: Here was a cowboy on a ten-dollar horse, riding on a five-dollar wooden saddle, and the rope he was using was made out of horsehair, but the one thing that really caught your eye was the fancy white shirt, and the ear-to-ear grin on this cowboy's face.

They were real cowboys. Their complete life had been dedicated to this business of raising beef, and they were good at it. I enjoyed watching them work cattle; it was more fun than a rodeo because they were fast and efficient, with an emphasis on the fast. My hangout, or at least, where I slept, was a bunkhouse about a mile from the Hacienda and close to the hangar. We had a fair-size staff from the ranch with the Boss, including Secret Service and the White House signal people. At night when the boss and his guests had retired, the off-duty personnel would have a little old poker game that lasted into the night––no high stakes, just fellowship.

In the middle of one dark night, and let me tell you, if the moon was absent, it was hard to see the back of your hand, the radio in the bunkhouse came alive. I was to get down to the Hacienda "pronto." Arriving at his bedroom, the Boss informed me that he was feeling poorly, but the reason he called me down was to make sure that I was there. He then said, "I damn sure don't want to die in Mexico." It was only a little indigestion, and it passed.

The electrical power for the Hacienda was furnished by a big outdated generator. Once in operation, it could be heard a mile away. I think maybe we took a standby down a little later to update the system. The Mexican staff had made do with very little, and they were very good at it. Somehow they had kept the obsolete equipment in operation. There was one man who did all this, and he was really something. He was always busy fixing this and that and painting. You name it, and he could do it. He was an electrician, country style, with no test equipment. To see if a wire was hot or not, he would wet his finger and swiftly touch the wire. If he jumped about a foot in the air, it was hot.

The Secret Service drove some of its vehicles from Texas to the ranch in Mexico. Harsh roadways took their toll on these vehicles. They would arrive, looking very much like they had come out of a war zone. Hubcaps were long gone, due to the large holes in the roadway; the automobiles were covered with a layer of dust and were loose in every joint. Even the folks who built them could not have put them through a more severe test. One of the cars had a hole knocked in the oil pan, and oil was escaping at a fast rate.

Hey, no sweat; our handyman ran it up on some chunks of wood, crawled under it, and welded it shut. Technology, education, and experience had paid off big time. The people on this ranch will always be in my memory. Give them some wire, and they would build a fence. Everything else they needed would come from the land. They had learned to make do with very little.

127

There were two more projects, which popped up, and the Boss jumped into them. He just could not sit around and relax. He had to have something going on, and of course that meant we, ranch hands, and everyone else, who were unlucky enough to be close at hand, were cranked up and put into motion to complete this new project.

One was a water well, which had been used to water a field, but now was not pumping. The other was a small bulldozer, abandoned by the Mexican Army after the airstrip was completed. You would think, wouldn't you, if the machine was worth hauling back to Mexico City, they would have dragged it back with the other equipment. Now many years later, we were going to put his piece of junk back into service. As the Boss said, it would be handy to have around the ranch. Parts were ordered and were to be sent from El Paso by bus to the little town that was close to the ranch. The big items like the cutting blade for the dozer, which weighed several hundred pounds, was picked up by yours truly in San Antonio and flown to the ranch. The irrigation well was cleaned up, and the engine that pulled the water out of its hiding place was tested and found to be satisfactory.

Now, on this project, all that remained was to get the seed bed ready and get the seed. This last task fell to me. The Boss wanted to plant Johnson grass, a real hardy grass, which can be grazed or put up as hay. As a matter of fact, at the ranch in Texas, we were always trying to kill it out, so I flew back to Texas to pick it up. I took out all of the passenger seats, and to keep my weight and balance correct, I stacked the bags of seed over the spar of the wing. To get into the cockpit, I had to crawl over the bags and through a very tiny opening to get to my place of business. It was a sure bet, if anything bad happened, it would be a slow exit from the aircraft.

After crossing the border, the weather turned sour on me. As a solid line of storms forced me to deviate from my course, I had to climb, climb, climb to try to clear the lowest part of the system. I finally got through the weather with a pretty decent ride, but later on, I started to worry about my passengers/cargo. People who stay above the magical ten thousand feet area without oxygen for a length of time, have some of their brain cells die on them. I knew that I was safe, as all the cells that I once maybe had, were long gone––but what about the seed? Had I killed the seed's germination quality? Believe me, when I tell you that I really sweated it out until I received word that it was growing and doing well.

I think the President really did enjoy the time that he spent down on this ranch in Mexico. It was peaceful, quiet, and people could not get to him unless he wanted it to happen. It was not any different than from Texas, other than the fact that we were in a foreign country.

With the well flowing, and the hay growing, his attention turned to the old worn-out bulldozer. "Get that damn old tractor working and productive."

So it was balls out to get this project completed.

It was a slow process; one thing was fixed, and another item was found to be bad. He tired of this and called for a military plane to come down and pick him up and take him to Virginia to visit his oldest daughter and family. His instructions to me were to stay until the dozer was running, and then return to Texas.

Either on the way to Virginia or shortly after, he suffered another heart attack. If I carried out his last orders, which I always did, I would have been doomed to stay forever in Mexico. The good Lord smiled down on us. The Boss recovered, and we got the bulldozer operating. He was to return to this hideaway in Mexico a number of times more in his lifetime.

I have tried to analyze what the attraction was to him. I knew what it was to me. It had peaceful and quiet surroundings, but for a man who had been President, one who ran our great country during a period of war and passionate civil strife, what did it mean to him? I finally decided that it went back to his roots. His grandfather put together large herds of cattle to be trailed to the north. He fought Indians and all the other hazardous conditions of the frontier. So just maybe in the back of his mind, with the genes exerting their influence, he was carving out an empire, not unlike his forbears.

He had made a magnificent dent in this culture on the ranch by setting into operation a Head Start school. Children would receive an education, unlike their parents, to prepare them for life beyond the valley and the ranch. He would copycat his life's work, which was helping the poor and the illiterate. It really meant a lot to him to be doing this. If you were to ask him why he was doing this, he might not have the answer, but he was making sure it was being carried out. The sad part was that he would not live to see the results of his efforts.

To further explain his intentions for the ranch, I will tell you that he had me pick up and fly a geologist from Texas Tech down to the ranch and stay with him until he completed his study of the water that lay underground in the valley. In his report to the Boss, he stated that the valley floor lay just above a lake of water. Fifty thousand acres could be irrigated by shallow wells. The Boss, in his mind, had this vision of miles and miles of truck farming at its best with food for everyone——but it was not to be. He told me later that it was hard to give up this project, but he believed he would not live to see it completed. He was right; he would not have seen the project in full swing.

One lazy summer day at the ranch in Mexico, the Boss asked me how long it would take me to fly to Santa Fe and pick up his brother-in-law and return to the ranch. He was not satisfied with my reply and wondered why it would take so long. I explained that stopping at Texas customs, coming and going, ate up a lot of time. This was something he could sink his teeth into. I do not think that the time element meant anything to him as we had settled into the Mexican "maybe tomorrow" mode, but a tiny challenge had appeared.

"I believe I appointed Mr. So and So, who is head of Texas Customs."

Our generator was cranked up, and the signal boys had this person on the line to talk to the Boss in two minutes. Boy, these people were good! They could locate you even if you had gone to Hell. As a matter of fact, they had found me a lot of times when I did not want to be found.

Well, anyhow, the headman at customs said I could over fly the border anytime I wanted. I was a believer by now, but this was one more example that my boss could do anything. Of course, in this time frame with our drug-crazy society, it would be difficult, but my money would still be on the Boss.

10

Tony Taylor, Mrs. Johnson's brother, was an interesting man. He had an import-export business in Santa Fe. On our return to the ranch, we flew at low level with this man pointing out and knowing the names of the towns and villages. He had traveled most of Mexico by car, mule, and on foot to conduct his business. We were later to meet all of his family, and they were lovely people.

All good things have to end sooner or later. I think of this ranch in Mexico even today. There were no traffic problems, no loud noises, not a lot of people to get in your way and take up your space. Now to a "do-gooder, people-lover" type, being sent to this ranch would seem like a passport to Devil's Island, but to an anti-social, anti-human, part-time redneck, like myself, I had found my heaven on earth. There are places like this left in the world, but eventually the tree huggers will bring them under their influence, and there goes the neighborhood. Seriously, I think the Boss really did enjoy his time spent on this ranch in the middle of nowhere. I know that I did.

For many years, the Boss had restrained from smoking on the advice of his medicos because of his heart condition. He had been a smoker and loved tobacco, and when I would forget and light up one of my cheap cigars around him, I would hear from him. "Barney, put that damn stinking thing out!"

Then, like a bolt from the blue, I would see him smoking a cigarette with the rest of the pack nestled in his shirt pocket. Things were different at our get-togethers. It would be, "Bring me an ashtray, and bring Barney one also." Every now and then, some really fine cigars would find their way to me, courtesy of my Boss.

Reflecting back on this, I believe that he made the decision to maybe shorten his life a tad in favor of something that gave him much pleasure. This would be very hard to explain to straight-laced folks, whose lips have never touched tobacco, so I won't even try. I also think that he had the mind-set that the end of the road was drawing near. He seemed to be doing exactly what he wanted to do, which sounds silly as hell, because most of his life, he had pretty much done as he liked, but now he seemed more deliberate in his activities.

We would fly to football games all around the state with the airplane loaded to the gills with his friends and neighbors. Fun times were here, and it was not the same group every time, but people we all knew. We had a ball, and the Boss had more fun than anyone.

On one occasion returning from a game, we had an intercom system that allowed the Boss to talk to me in the cockpit, and my reply would be heard by everyone in the cabin. It was fun for him, although not too much fun for me.

I was to hear this through my headset, "Barney, do you have any of those chocolate covered Oreos that I like so much?" My negative response was answered with, "Do you have any cheese and crackers?"

Being more than knowledgeable about his diet, my response had to be, "No, Sir."

A short pause followed by, "Damn it, don't you have anything to eat on this airplane?"

My negative answer was followed by, "You are fired."

If I had been blessed with mucho gonads, I would have pulled the thrust levers back and gone into a steep decent, which I am sure would have sparked this comment from the Boss into my earpiece, "What in the hell are you doing?"

My reply could have been, "Well, you just fired me, so I am going to land and get out."

That would have been going too far and never forgiven.

On one occasion returning from a game late at night, with level flight in the mid-twenties, the cabin door seal failed, and we lost our pressurized cabin. It made a sound like a gun going off. The Secret Service agent, who always sat in the jump seat at the rear of the airplane, told me later that immediately ten pairs of eyes looked at him as if to say, "Hey, dummy, why did you fire your weapon?"

I called center and requested a lower altitude, which was granted, and I got down where we could breathe and the brain cells would quit dying.

From the first air that we pull into our lungs at birth, we have started our first step on our journey to the very end of our cycle on this earth. God will decide how long and how hard that trip will be. We should do our very best to please the Almighty and to follow His teachings. I am positive that He is disappointed in our endeavors, but just maybe, the fact that we did believe, might put us in good standing in the world beyond.

What a Christmas this was! The ranch hands, the SS, and their families were all gathered together in the hangar as we had been for past Christmases. From outside we could hear the sound of a small engine running in the idle position. The side doors of the hangar suddenly opened and in came Santa Claus riding on a lawn mower. It was the Boss dressed as Old Saint Nick. He gave the riding lawn mower to Father Schneider, the local priest, and then Mr. Claus proceeded to give out toys, along with a five-dollar bill, to the little boys and girls. He had miscalculated the number of children who were present, so he had to ask Mike Howard, his head SS agent, for a few more bills. It was one Christmas I will never forget, and it was the last one that we would celebrate with him.

This Sunday in January was not unlike other weekends in which we always seemed to be moving around the country, but it would change my life forever. I had the aircraft full of ranch hands, whom I was taking to northeast Nebraska to attend a course on irrigation. When we arrived there, we were in the middle of a snowstorm. I finally found the airport and the runway, and after landing, I got as close to the old buildings, (which I imagine they would call hangars), and dumped the ranch hands and their baggage into a snow bank. It was not an easy take-off because the snow was deep, but without the weight, which I had just dropped, I was able to get airborne, and a few minutes later, I was above the storm and flying in smooth air.

By the time I was over southern Kansas it was late, and I was ready to call it a day. I landed at Wichita, Kansas, which had excellent facilities. Their specialty was a fast turn-around, and I had used them a lot in the past. They would almost be pumping fuel before the props stopped turning. I landed on an ice-covered runway with a stiff crosswind, which did its best to blow me off the runway. By using the differential power of the engines, I was able to taxi to the parking area. I was more than ready to unsaddle this old horse.

It had been a long day with bad weather all the way. There was a motel right at the airport, so I grabbed my bag and got a ride over to it. I walked in and went over to the desk to make arrangements. Before I could get in a "Howdy," the clerk wanted to know if I was Barney from the L.B.J. Ranch in Texas. To my affirmative, she stated that I was to call the ranch right away.

My hide began to crawl like it had done before when I was in a tight spot. Something must have happened to a member of my family. Why else would the White House signal its operatives to run me down in the middle of the night? I did not even know I was coming here until the very last minute. My original plan was to go to Fort Smith, Arkansas, where I was to pick up milk producers early the next morning and take them to a meeting in San Antonio. However, like I have said before, those men sitting in that little mobile house could find you even if you had gone to hell. Later, I found out that they went through the flight service to track me down. Once they knew where I had landed, they then went to the fix base operator to see where I had gone after that. Simple, is it not?

I rushed to a phone and called these people who had deftly "treed" yours truly. They informed me that the President wanted to talk to me and connected me right away. The Boss told me that he had been watching the weather, and it looked bad up there in Nebraska, and when he had tried to contact the ranch hands, he had no luck. He said that he was really worried about us, and he could not go to sleep until he knew we were safe and sound. I told him that I had dropped them off, but they probably had some trouble getting into the motel because of the storm.

He also asked if Tom Mills had been on the plane. I told him that he had been. To which he replied, "Hell, I did not want him to go up there."

Tom was a Navy corpsman whose job was looking after the health of the President. Like everyone else, he did a lot of other things. He was our very own private doctor, and if anyone anywhere on the ranch needed help, Tom was there to add another helping hand.

His next words were, "Where in the hell are you?"

I told him where I was, and that in a few hours I would be heading for Fort Smith to pick up the milk people to take them to San Antonio. I could picture his mind going over the facts that part of the cost of this trip would be picked up by our friends. With a "God bless you," the connection was broken.

A few hours later, I rolled out of a nice warm bed and pulled on my boots, not knowing that it would be twenty-four hours plus, before the boots would come off, and I would be in a nice warm bed again. I made the pick-up at Fort Smith in time. The milk people were always on time, especially on early morning flights. Maybe the habit of getting up early to milk the cows was hard to break. After arriving in San Antonio, as was their custom, they asked me to go with them to corporate headquarters and then to have lunch with them. I was to take them back home at four P.M., but for some reason, which I will never know, I declined their offer. I told them that I was going out to the ranch to service the aircraft.

After arriving at the ranch, I did not go to lunch in nearby Stonewall, and I did not service the aircraft. I just went into the Secret Service shack and plopped into a chair with my feet up to watch the world go by. This was our world at the ranch—a large picture window with a view of the main house, surveillance cameras for all the gates and roads leading to the complex. Two-way radios, telephones, and a teletype completed this security arrangement. I knew it like the back of my hand. Out of the twenty-one years that I worked there, it seemed like I had spent one year in this shack either waiting on one of my bosses to go somewhere, or on stand-by, or sometimes just loafing there and visiting with my friends. We got to know each other pretty well in that period of time.

My relaxed status was interrupted by the hot line, which was a direct line from the main house to the Secret Service shack. It was picked up by the shift leader with a "Yes, Sir," as a response.

It was loud enough that I could hear the, "Get in here, boys. I need help."

The two agents ran as hard as they could to the main house and disappeared into it. It seemed like an eternity, but it was only a minute or two, when the shift leader's voice broke the radio's silence with a, "Looks like it's going sour on us."

All hell broke loose. Telephones were manned, and radio commo was going full bore.

As I left the shack, I told someone that I would get my engines fired up. The forty-yard distance from the shack to the aircraft was covered by me in giant leaps. My stand-by duty in helicopters for the White House was paying off. I took a shortcut through the starting procedure and lit the fires. Then I made an unnecessary radio call to the command post to let them know I was in place and ready. The noise from the turbines would have already disclosed that fact.

In just a minute or two, around the corner of the hangar came a fearful sight. The President was on a litter, supported by Secret Service agents, ranch hands, and house personnel. He was lifted into the aircraft, but he could not be moved forward because of the narrow passageway. I had power up and was starting to move when an automobile arrived in the fast mode. It was the doctor from Johnson City, who had risked his life and probably lives of others on the road, to get to the ranch in a short time. With power up to the max, we were airborne, and I gave a shout to the passengers to move forward as I was out of trim and headed south to San Antonio.

I had radio contact with San Antonio approach control. An emergency was declared, and as soon as I was identified on their radar, I was cleared to land on any available runway of my choice. The controllers always did a good job at San Antonio, but this time they really did show off. We had gone ground to ground in twelve minutes with all the gauges at the bottom of the red line. An ambulance and medical people were at the ramp and boarded as soon as the door went down. I stayed in my seat, as time seemed to come to a standstill. No one was in a hurry anymore. Everyone's face had a grim look. My worst fears had come true. My Boss was gone.

Mrs. Johnson arrived in a short time. She had been in Austin and was put on a military helicopter for a fast trip to San Antonio. I watched the chopper land on the ramp, and as she off-loaded, my heart went out to her and to the family. I was so very, very sorry for her, the family, and even for me. I had lost not only the man who had hired me and trusted me with everything including his life and the lives of his family, but I had lost a friend, whom I really believed cared about the welfare of me and mine. As I look back now, I would have to say it was one of the saddest days of my life.

I went to Mrs. Johnson, and of course, words failed me. Being the strong person that she is and caring for others as she does, she told me to take those people, who needed to return to the ranch. About this time, the milk people had spotted the airplane and came to it even though it was not at our regular terminal.

When they had been informed of what had happened, their response was, "Don't worry about us. We will make our own way home." What understanding people they were.

I went back to the ranch with those who had to return. Then I made a dash home to tell Libby, who had already seen it on T.V. A short time later a call came in from Mrs. Johnson to tell me that she hated to ask me to do it, but she thought it best if we got our people out of Nebraska. I got our people on the horn and asked them if they could meet me in Omaha because I just knew that the run way at Norfolk would be ass deep with snow. It worked out just right. As they finished pumping me full of Jet A., they drove in. The flight back home to Texas was the saddest and quietest trip I have ever made. Each person lost in his own thoughts and thinking of their loss.

As I think back in time, some thoughts come back to me. Whenever the President would try to get hold of me on his radio, and could not reach me for various reasons, I would soon hear about it. It was always the same. "Damn it, Barney, some day I will really need you, and you will not be there."

This time when he might have needed me, I will never know why, but I was there. I had landed an hour or so before, so he knew that I was at the ranch. He had always told me that whether early or late, he was the one who heard me coming and leaving. Like no one else heard, just him, and he was the only one who would give a damn that I was safe and sound.

But, why was I there? What power had sent me back to the ranch, when it would have been so easy to stay in town and have a great lunch, while someone pumped the fuel into the airplane? I will never know the answer to this, but I thank God that it did happen that way. I felt so sorry for my friend, the shift leader, that day. He was one of the favorites of the President with loyalty and respect going both ways. My friend had to stay in town that night and observe the autopsy of the President's body. It was said death came swiftly. One side of the heart had exploded, and even if it had happened on the operating table, they could not have saved him.

The body of this great man was flown to our nation's capital to lie in state in the rotunda of the capitol building. He had served on both sides of this great building. Thousands and thousands of citizens stood quietly in long lines to file by and say their good-byes and show their respect for this former President of our nation. So many of us will always be indebted to him because of his yearning for all to obtain and to forever keep their civil rights.

Also, it was his desire to help people out of poverty, which in turn, would enhance his dream for everyone to receive a good education. This went back, I am sure, to his days as a schoolteacher in a financially poor area in South Texas. So much more would have been accomplished by this man if he had not been driven from a second term because of the Vietnam War and the riots, which were partially initiated by young people who did not want to serve their country but wanted to reap all of the benefits of a free society.

To those, who left the country during this period to keep from serving in Vietnam, I say to you, your actions are not to warrant any forgiveness. In fact, your mind-set could have helped to start the "Me" instead of "We" generation, which has slowly decayed the morality of us all. I will now step down from the pulpit, but what I wanted to do was defend this great man, who had just left us to our sorrow.

The President's body was then transported back to the capital of his home state and to the L.B.J. Library, into which I am sure, he gave input regarding the supervision of this project. Libby and I were able to join the endless lines of people from Texas. The day arrived with the commitment of his body to the earth of his beloved ranch.

It was a bad day––not that any day would have been good––but weather-wise it bordered on being miserable. It was almost down to the freezing mark, with a light rain falling that could not make up its mind whether it wanted to be a fluid or a solid. A mass of people tried to get as close as they could to this little private cemetery. A military honor guard from Fort Sam Houston, plus truck-loads of soldiers for traffic and crowd control added to this sea of humanity. People were parking their wheels across the river on Ranch Road 1 and walking one-half mile to join the others. It was a very solemn and reverent group of people who were present on this bleak day. Mrs. Johnson, as always so thoughtful, had the ranch hands moved into the walled enclosure to stand with the family. We were so close to Dr. Billy Graham that we could almost reach out and touch him. With the eulogies over, this great man's body was to be laid to rest only one hundred yards from where he had come into this world. He had made his mark in history, and in some of us, he left a sadness that will linger forever.

The world was still turning, and our lives had to go on. As he would have said, "Get high behind and get on with it."

11

I T WAS SO QUIET EVERYWHERE now that the Boss had left us. The ranch was not the same, and never would be the same. It was very hard to deal with. We were in a daze or a "zombie like" trance. Our actions were listless, our behavior was mechanical. This went on for a few days, and then like a snap of the finger, we came out of it, and we got on with our lives and got down to business. The milk people still had us on contract for almost two years with the option of more, so I went back to flying for them. I had enjoyed very much working for them, and things were not going to change in that part of my life.

Mrs. Johnson did not want to continue the cattle operation, so the cattle were gathered up, and we had a big cattle auction. In the back pasture was a small herd of Longhorns, which had been given to the President, or acquired in some fashion. These were descendants of the cattle of one hundred years ago, who walked all the way to Kansas just to be eaten. These cows had not been worked with or domesticated in any way. They roamed their little range, just like their forefathers. They were not really wild, but they were doing what they wanted to do.

One of them, a very old steer, whose teeth had worn off, was in bad shape. You could count every rib bone, including the short one, and he had a terrible-looking fungus growing on his back that looked like moss. Anyway, Mrs. Johnson saw him and asked me to please send him to Longhorn heaven. It was hard for me to do, but I did it. I like animals and have not done anything like that since. I do not hunt the deer but enjoyed feeding them in the wintertime and watching them eat.

Mrs. Johnson also likes to watch the wildlife, the Longhorns, and the wildflowers when in season. She also liked to make this pilgrimage, especially if she had been absent for a while, so that she could see and make sure that everything was doing all right. She decided that our Longhorn herd was getting too large for the grass we had, so it was decided that we would sell some. That task fell to me to dispose of the surplus. From that time on, fun and games ended, and the rodeo began.

Now picture if you can, animals who have done exactly what they pleased all of their lives and had never been exposed to the human species, other than being fed during the winter months. Plus, there was one bull, who tried to impale me on the end of his horns every time I fed him. I finally decided that this renegade was not going to get me. I would open up a bag of cubes before I found the herd and then pour them out as I drove along. This worked well. He got fed, and I did not have to get behind a tree.

Getting them in a pen, where we could load them out, would test my ingenuity. I hauled a round bale of hay into the middle of the pen, and let greed take its course. When I had most of them in the enclosure, I closed the gate. They did not like this much, especially old belligerent, but we had already decided that we would tranquilize this sucker before we tried to load him. We hit him with the dart from a gun, and down he went, right on top of the pile of hay. His eyes rolled, and his ears fell down by the side of his head. We had given him too much, and he was in another world. We proceeded with loading the others, and it was not a pretty sight.

Dumb old us. We thought that once we had a rope on them, we could drag them into the stock trailer with a horse. Guess again. We ended up pulling them in with another truck, and that was not easy. We saved the best for last, and finally got old toughie loaded as he was coming out of his fog. At the auction barn, I told the guys to keep an eye on them, as they were a little wild. They informed me that they had handled mean cattle before, and they knew what they were doing. From the reports I received, one or two of the guys almost got wiped out when our horns got into the ring.

A week or so later I took some other cattle in, and the first thing they said was, "Don't bring any more of those damn Longhorns in to us."

Now that the Boss had left me, I was completely surrounded by females. The President's grandson was in school, and I was all by myself and completely at their mercy. They dominated me at work and at home. (Just kidding, I really do like females.) To demonstrate my attentive and considerate nature towards females, I truly believe that there were only two times in my entire life that I did not return the toilet seat to the down position. They had my full support when they started the feminist movement, and they still do.

I was agitated when there was no outcry from them when the "Bubba and the Intern" episode came to light. By not getting really exercised about this, I fear they have taken a step back in their movement. They will still have to work hard to retain and gain their battle for equality.

The women in my life have been a source of joy to me, starting with my wife, who has stayed by my side for fifty-three years. People who really know me would tell you that she has to be a unique person to have put up with me for such a long period of time. Our daughters turned out just fine, and they bring much pride to us. Now to the fun part . . . the granddaughters . . . it is to them I have dedicated this story. They, by being born in our later years, would not know of our history in the beginning of our family. We do not have any grandsons, just five very intelligent and pretty granddaughters. At first, this bothered me a little bit, but even as slow as I am, I soon figured out that girls could do anything that boys could, and in most cases, they do it much better. The good Lord knows, they are so much prettier to look at.

The women in President Johnson's family also added some additional spice to my life. I am so happy that we are friends and will be until the end of our time. Claudia Taylor Johnson, who is the most gracious, caring, and family-oriented person, was to become my number one boss. She has so many sterling qualities that pop into my mind at this time, but there was a slight crack in this dam built upon solid rock. She was uneasy about flying in general, due to an unhappy experience in the past, so bouncing around in rough weather with rain and lightning would terrify her. I felt so sorry for her because of the many commitments she had; she almost had to put herself through the wringer so to speak. We planned many flights, and we completed most of them, but now and then we would get on the edge of a storm, and it would get rough.

Her call to me would always be the same, "Land anywhere that you can, and we will take the bus."

(I think that in the back of her mind she knew that the SS agents would not put her on a bus even if they had to hot-wire a vehicle out of the airport parking lot.)

Over the years we went to a lot of places in the USA and Mexico, and it was fun and enjoyable. We flew to many of the national parks to visit and observe, and this thoughtful and charming lady would always invite Libby to go along.

At this point in time, the L.B.J. National Historic site had a female superintendent, who was intelligent enough to find the value of having Libby, who was a personal friend of Mrs. "J" and also an employee of the park bearing her husband's name, take part in these trips. Libby was encouraged to accompany whenever invited.

This was to change dramatically in the future when jealousy and pettiness set in with the higher-ups in the local park. They were resentful of Libby's relationship with Mrs. J. In this time frame, picture this if you will; there was a female superintendent, who told me face-to-face that she was a Vietnam anti-war demonstrator from Berkeley University. The second-in-command was a man, whose family was banned from setting foot on the L.B.J. Ranch. I am sure my former Boss was turning over in his grave.

I, and many others, had heard the former President state on many occasions that he did not want the visitors to be charged money to tour the ranch. He said that the poor people with big families would want to tour and any fee would deter them. Well, at this time, three dollars per head is being levied on those who would like to take the Ranch tour. I am sure that there was another outcry from the grave.

It seems strange to me that the national park service, which can always find money for their projects, would countermand the wishes of this great man, who along with Mrs. Johnson, gave the Interior Department the land and the sites which stood on this land. If there is justification for this procedure, I would be happy to hear it. I would give you odds, that if this man was still with us, this procedure would not be in effect. The statement that he made in this regard, in the last years of his time here, tells me that he was still thinking of the poor people. Well, off of my soapbox and back to more pleasant thoughts.

Luci, Luci, Luci! A warm, generous, religious, family-oriented person, the daughter of President and Mrs. Johnson. After the death of her father, she was appointed (or she volunteered) to be the President of the Heart Association of Texas. She wanted to talk to as many people as she could about this affliction that had taken her father, and she wanted me to fly her. It was rock and roll time. No town was too small. If they had an airstrip 3,000 feet or longer, we were there. When we first started these trips, she would come to the cockpit after take-off and practice her speech on me. On later trips, whenever she made changes in her talk, she would try the new lines out on me again. Toward the last of this period, I truly believe I could have gone by myself and given the talk, but then I would have missed out on some fun, and it was fun. Here was a person who had absolutely no fear of flying. It was a joy and a pleasure to fly her. She must have truly believed that God and her outstanding pilot would see her safely home.

I could never pinpoint why this would happen, but when on the few occasions it did, it was usually fairly late in the evening. I would get this call from my favorite passenger about being stuck somewhere and having no way home. She would ask, "Can you come and get me?"

It would not have been too bad if she had been somewhere in the state of Texas, but several times she was in other states. I would have to point my finger at her secretary and give her credit for getting Luci somewhere and not planning a way back home.

I was always meeting her at some of the big airports when she flew in, and then I would take her back to Austin. I would position myself where I could observe every person who would off-load. She would be looking around as she deplaned, and when she saw me, a big smile would come on her face. Then I devised this plan of standing behind an obstacle where I would see her, without her spotting me. After she had looked around for her security blanket for a minute or two, I would step out and get my hug. What an evil thing to do to anyone. Luci, if by chance you should read this, my defense would have to be that the devil made me do it. Hours of boredom, waiting around airports, will finally mess up your mind. I am not sure about this, but I might have been the very first person in the world to call in a bomb threat at an airport. Just kidding, but boredom did influence me to take up needlepoint.

There was another time when I met her flight in Dallas on a very cold winter night. It was one of those last-flights-into-Dallas-with-no-flight-into-Austin deals. We arrived in Austin in the wee hours about half past the witching hour. With the baggage in tow, I escorted my passenger to the airport parking lot. She had three vehicles available to her, so I asked her which one she had driven to the airport. I feel safe in telling this because since then, I have reminded her of the incident. She did not remember which car she had driven, so we started looking for any of the above. It was really cold, and I knew she was cold, even though she had a big fur coat to cover part of her. I had passed from the cold stage to numbness. The parking lot was the size of an east Texas ranch, so we split up to cover more territory. I was about to throw in the towel when, for a split second, I thought that a grizzly bear had me around the neck.

I was to hear these words, "Oh, Barney, I'm so sorry. I just remembered that I came to the airport in a taxi."

And that is the way she went home that cold dark morning.

I had the habit of writing down the number of the vehicle I put her in, and not that it would do her any good, but at least I would know where I last saw her. The world is full of nutsos and the population is growing.

If, and heaven forbid, it would come about, and I were to find myself in the "one-call" position, I would call Luci. She is a person of loyalty to friends and causes that she believes in. Also, when she starts something, she is very much like the bulldog that sinks his teeth into you and will not quit until he has eaten you. She has devoted a lot of time, energy, and resources to younger people who were suffering from dyslexia. Early in her life she had gone through this herself, and she knew a lot about it and the effects it had on young people.

When I brag on her and her accomplishments, some people will reply, "It is easy to do this when you have money." Hell's bells——I know of many people with money who only help themselves. Case closed.

Somewhere in this time frame, while on vacation in the Cayman Islands, she met a man from Scotland, who had a position in one of the four hundred banks in Georgetown. During this courtship, I was to make many trips there. It was not as easy as you might think because it was hard to receive reliable weather down there. After a trip or two, I met a policeman who appeared to run the airport; I got his number, and before any trip started, I would call him and get the weather. Now, with the weather satellites, it would be so easy.

We would leave the USA mainland at Galveston and fly six hundred miles over water to the island of Cozumel, and then back over water to the Caymans. If the weather in the Caymans was bad, I could return to

Cozumel or go east to Montego Bay, Jamaica. This last leg of the flight was through Cuban airspace. Sometimes they would answer our radio calls and give us a clearance, and sometimes they would not. When the latter happened, I fully expected to look out of the cockpit and see a MIG fighter on our wingtip. In all my trips to the Caymans, I lucked out and always got in. I might add that Luci had some good luck and married this super guy.

Ian Turpin is a real gentleman in every sense of the word. They were joined together in the West Room of the Texas White House. I was invited but declined because I would have had to suit up in a tux. I will regret this until two days before they throw dirt on my final resting place. My favorite passenger reminds me of this on most occasions, and it also pops up now and then in my thoughts. I did later acquire a tux and wore it on special occasions, like on some of the cruise ships we were on.

Early on we had decided that as soon as Libby retired from her job with the park that we would travel while we were both in good health and mobile. We had known so many couples who kept putting it off––until something happened to one of them, and then the remaining mate would just sit around and complete none of their travel plans. Not us.

Mrs. Johnson and I had made "the last hurrah," as she called it, with a trip back to her roots in Alabama. I retired to a peaceful life of ranching. Often when I am asked why I hung it up when I did, I bring to mind what Dirty Harry would say, "You have to know your limitations." Forty-five years of flying would be enough.

So one summer it was off to Alaska and the next summer to Australia and New Zealand. The next year we were off to southeast Asia by the way of Tokyo, Japan, and then on to Bangkok, Thailand, where we toured most of this beautiful country. Then we were on to Singapore, which is one of the cleanest and prettiest cities in the world. There we met our cruise ship, which was the same one on which we had explored New Zealand. Then it was on to Malaya and into Kuala Lumpur for a visit. I even found the tall round building where I had stayed for President Johnson's visit. We were then back plowing through the South China Sea to dock again in Saigon, now called Ho Chi Minh City. We spent a day down in the Delta. We had a good time and enjoyed eating the fish, which were taller than they were long, and other foods that we could not identify but were very tasty. We also went to an island in the Mekong River to look at the new plants they were growing. A storm came up as we were leaving the island. Boy, it was nip and tuck getting back across to the other side. What a large river with waves like you see on an ocean––or so it seemed in that small boat.

Back on the ship, we went on up to Da Nang, my home away from home. Not much had changed in twenty-seven years except there was more traffic and more people. Some of the people seemed to be better off and some did not. I talked to an ex-Cong, who told me that the government was allowing them to own a business, but the taxes were very high. I guess they did learn something from us.

Libby and I, with the others from the ship, loaded into an air-conditioned van and set off on our tour. We passed the Da Nang airport, which seemed so strangely quiet now. We went through the downtown area, where I looked for but could not find the villa where I lived during the first part of my tour. Then we were on to Highway 1 and northbound over the pass, which I previously wrote about. That is enough said about this area where many lives were lost. Ghosts of the fallen will haunt this pass forever.

We then went down the other side and in to the flatland, where I could find no changes from the years before. The women still planted rice while the men plowed the rice paddies with water buffalo. We went on past the old airstrip at Phu Bai and into Hue. Hue is a royal city dominated by the massive Citadel, where powerful emperors who ruled this city lived for more than a century. During the TET offensive, the North Vietnamese raised their flag over the Citadel. I worked over this area for a period of time because it was very difficult for our forces to regain control. This was a rerun of our Civil War with kinfolk killing kinfolk. I could not tell from the air, but it was reported that the Perfume River was full of bodies. Finally, we were in control at a high price on both sides.

It looked so peaceful this day that Libby and I were there, and the North Vietnamese flag was back, flying high over the Citadel. We had lunch in the best and oldest hotel in the city. All of the staff were dressed as they would have been in the days of the Emperor. What a delightful day without hearing a single shot being fired!

Back to the ship, we were on to the north to Halong Bay, and one of the world's scenic wonders. There are three thousand limestone islets stretched over about 3,500 square miles. Caves and grottoes riddle these islands. We dropped the hook in a beautiful spot and off-loaded into junks and small boats to explore this world treasure. It was a fun day, and one we will remember forever.

Back aboard our floating home, we sailed between the China mainland and the now famous island of Hainan to Hong Kong. China really does have a lot of offshore oil and gas, which we could see from the ship, and by the way, Vietnam exports oil.

Hong Kong, the commercial hub of southeast Asia, is a fascinating place to see, but do not take your wife there to shop. They move at two paces in this town––fast and faster. We did enjoy looking around the shops and markets and seeing the world's largest floating restaurant. We took a trip to the top of the Victoria Peak, where you could look over all of Hong Kong, and at night it was spectacular. We decided that before we left Hong Kong we would go to Macau, an island that had been founded by the Portuguese. They were still there and running everything. We have seen a lot of islands, but deep down we wanted to ride on a jetfoil boat and hit the big casinos. We enjoyed the boat ride, and the tour wasn't bad, but it took longer than it was supposed to, and by the time we arrived at the casino, it was late, and the Chinese were lined up three deep to wager. We had found someone who liked to gamble as much as we did, so it was back to our hotel in Hong Kong. The next day we were on our way back home.

We were to venture forth again to explore the fascinations of civilizations past. We flew to Miami and boarded an Air Alitalia 747, and we were on to Rome. What a flight that was! We were two of fourteen people who were up in the very top of the aircraft. The service we received was from another world. We received a seven-course meal with real silver and linens and several kinds of wine. We had been spoiled on Qantas Airlines when we went down under––but not like this! On Qantas, there appeared to be a quota on the bottles of wine that had to be consumed each flight. They would wake you up in the morning before breakfast and offer wine to drink. With our position being shown on the T.V. screen, we knew where we were at all times. We went from Miami up over Long Island, New York, to Paris and into Rome. Hard to believe that is the shortest route, but it is.

We changed aircraft and flew to Athens, Greece. Customs and security had been very strict in Rome, but in Athens, these procedures were non-existent. I could have had one of my baby calves with me and escaped unnoticed. We spent some time exploring this great city. What stands out, and it can be seen from almost anywhere in the city, is the Acropolis. It is a mute testament to the golden age of Pericles, which produced some of the greatest artists, architects, philosophers, and writers the world has ever known. This was an encounter with legacies of a culture that forged the very roots of Western Civilization, and Libby and I made the most of it. We walked and climbed through the Olympic Stadium, which is made of pentelic marble and was built in 1895 for the first Olympic games. We also walked and climbed the stairs made out of marble to really see the Acropolis. At nightfall, we returned to observe a play that was presented. The lighting and sound effects put you right on the scene, somewhat like our great production of *Texas* at Canyon. A lot of the buildings in Athens are old, and some are ancient, but all are very pretty. This was spoiled somewhat when we looked out the hotel window, and in the middle of all these aged structures was a modern-day McDonald's.

The next morning found us putting our bags outside our room in the hallway, and we retained only what hand items we wanted to carry on our person. This had been the procedure on all our trips. I always conducted a formal good-bye to the bags because deep down in my heart, I was afraid we would never meet again, but like the good penny, they would be in our next hotel room or stateroom on the ship. We never lost a single bag in all our overseas travel, but on domestic flights, in our own country, we have lost some and had others delayed. Kinda makes you think a little, does it not?

We loaded up on our bus and spent the day touring the Greek countryside. At the end of this day, we were at a seaport, and there was our ship. This would be the third time we had sailed on her in different parts of the world. It looked good, like our home away from home. We spent the next few days in the Greek Islands, docking at some and making short excursions. They were all a little different and not all had the same history. The part of the trip we had been anticipating, with much expectation, was really going to come about. We docked in Haifa, Israel.

Haifa, which is Israel's major seaport on the Mediterranean, looked like most industrial cities until you looked upward and saw the golden dome of the Bahai Temple rising above the slopes of Mount Carmel. This is also the place where David killed Goliath, and Jesus gave his sermon on the Mount. It was hard for us to believe we were right there. Israel is a tiny nation, yet its soil is holy to the world's three great religions—Judaism, Christianity, and Islam. We were starting our journey of place-names that echo those of the Bible. It was great. It made you feel at peace with yourself and your Maker. You feel so close to your forever home. It was so emotional, even for me, one who has dedicated his whole life in covering up the same.

While still in Haifa, we had the opportunity to visit the sacred sites of Galilee, which is now a blossoming resort area. The next day found us following the coastline to Tel Aviv and then on to Jerusalem. Along the roadway were old war machines, which had been hit and could go no further. The Israelis had left them there as a grim reminder to those who would invade this tiny nation that they will not return to their homeland. In the distance, you could see the Golan Heights, which is the main source of fresh water available to Israel. When we were there, they had one plant in operation to convert seawater to potable water, but I would have to guess they have more now.

Jerusalem. We were finally there in the old city founded by King David some 3,000 years ago, where Jesus was crucified and Mohammad rose to heaven. What a thrill that was for us! We visited the Church of the Holy Sepulcher, whose site marks Golgotha (also called Calvary), which is believed to be the place of Jesus' crucifixion, burial, and resurrection. Mere words cannot describe what we were feeling at this time. We visited the Western Wall, also called the wailing wall, which really is a retaining wall for Temple Mount. What an experience that was! The men went to the left portion of the wall to say their prayers, and the women went to the right. Libby had written her prayer on a piece of paper, which she stuffed into a crack in the wall, along with the many other pieces of paper that were already there. When you stood before this wall, you could hear prayers in almost every language. I cannot describe with words my feelings for this day, but I do know that I will never forget this experience.

Two weeks before we had departed on this trip, they had killed about seventy people at Temple Mount in a fire fight between the Israelis and Palestinians, so we were not sure if we could visit Bethlehem, which is controlled by the Palestinians. When we arrived in their area, they had roadblocks set up, but they just waved us through. Bethlehem is the Biblical setting for a lot of events, which includes the discovery of the shepherd, David, the future king of Israel, but its greatest significance is being the birthplace of Jesus. We got to see everything, including the oldest continuously used church in the world.

We had seen so many things on this leg of the trip, which included a two-thousand-year-old olive orchard, which grew out of rock and was still productive. All good things have to come to an end, so it was back to our floating home.

When we told people of our trip, they often asked if we were fearful at any time. I told them, "No, because nearly everyone was armed with a weapon."

Israeli law states that every able-bodied citizen, both male and female, will serve a term in the active reserve. During this time, they must have immediate access to their weapon. It was strange for us to observe a pretty young lady, dressed in the latest fashion, on her way to the office or university, boarding a bus with a light machine gun slung over her shoulder. These people have learned valuable lessons the hard way over the last fifty years.

I truly believe that the people of Israel are God's chosen few, and He has allowed so many bad things to happen to them, including the Holocaust, to teach the rest of His children a lesson. I hope we may learn from this.

After departing Haifa, we sailed to Turkey with several stops to go ashore and tour points of interest. One such stop was Troy, which I remembered from one of the times when I was awake in my history class. It had intrigued me then, thinking how devious the Greeks were and how gullible the people of Troy had been to drag that horse through their gates. A replica of the famous Trojan horse is the first thing you see on the site.

We sailed on up the Dardanelles, the narrow straits that separate Europe from Asia Minor. These straits and the area around it have a history of conflict for control of these vital waterways that goes back to 404 B.C. when the Spartans defeated the Athenians. There is so much history here, and in our travels, Libby and I had been exposed to much more history. Now, how much we absorbed will remain unknown, but we had a lot of fun and enjoyment poking around this old planet. I do regret playing hooky from school and history class to go to the pool hall to shoot pool. In my defense, I will say that I became a pretty fair stick man.

Istanbul——the city that spans two continents and creates scenes right out of the pages of *Tales of the Arabian Nights*. We tried to see everything in the few days permitted to us, and we did a pretty good job of it. We visited the Blue Mosque, where everyone had to leave their footwear outside. Hundreds of pairs of shoes were lined up outside the Mosque. When returning from prayer, the trick was to find your own shoes, or at the very least, find a pair that fit your feet and were comfortable. Also, the palaces with the Sultan's harems, from which my traveling companion barred me, were very interesting. This was the very same person who had me black-listed on the belly dancing. Istanbul also has the world famous Grand Bazaar, a maze of approximately 5,000 shops divided into sections according to their different trades. If you can't find it here, it does not exist.

From our balcony at the hotel, we watched a Europe/Asia marathon go down the street. It seemed to be endless with thousands of runners going by. I guess they were saying good-bye to us as the next morning in the dark with a cool rain falling, we departed Istanbul for Rome and then home.

We have one more trip in the planning stage. We would like to return to Münich, Germany, where we lived for four years during the Cold War and where we spent a small part of our happy life. Yes, we were happy, even under trying conditions. Military families go through phases of good times and bad times that parallel with assignments and reassignments. Those who truly love each other will endure through thick and thin and will still be together when the final taps is blown. We have known spouses, who were miserable regardless of where they were stationed. They hated the military and everything about their life. Of course, a few of these would find fault with heaven when and if they were to get there. The old saying, "You can't go back," is probably true, but we expect that everything has changed in forty-five years. It would be nice but also bad if no progress had been achieved in that time frame. So the good Lord willing, we will go back.

Libby and I count our blessings each day and thank our Savior for bestowing them upon us. We have so many to be thankful for: a wonderful family, many friends, our good health, and of course, the memory of our togetherness. Two, young, very much in love country kids created a family and nurtured it through to the very end. What more could we possibly ask for during our time here on earth?

A friend once asked me, "Why would you title the story of your earth life *Twenty Bosses*?" He went on to remark, "What's the big deal? I've had at least twenty jobs in my lifetime."

I had to explain to him that there was a period of time when I had all twenty at the same time. Just about anyone could call me, tell me where to go, and how to get there. Family members, upper echelon of our company, secretaries, and at times, even the SS would give me missions. In all fairness to myself, I tried my best to please everyone. There was only one of me and one airplane. Many a time, I wished for a time machine so that I could move everyone to where they wanted to be, but it was fun, and I enjoyed every part of it.

Mr. Webster defines "marriage" as the "state of being married, a relation between husband and wife, the rite or form used in marrying, any close or intimate union."

I have always believed in the vows that we said to each other before a person of God, especially the part that said to take care of your mate through good health and that sick stuff. In this time frame, the younger people do not seem to pay very much attention to their vows. If they get just a little bit unhappy with their mate, they pack up and pull out. Even in the best of marriages, there are some ups and downs. I have always heard that marriage is a series of give and take. I know that is correct, but I will guarantee, that in nearly all marriages, each partner will truly believe that he or she gives more than he or she takes.

Maybe we can squeeze some wisdom out of this. Libby and I have always thought that our marriage was stable and smooth running. We encountered a slight bump in the road when we were both retired and together at home. We discovered we were not compatible; we did not like the same T.V. programs. She liked the old movies and game shows. I enjoyed the ones with sex and violence, but we solved this problem with another set in another room.

This was of concern to our youngest daughter, who is self-appointed to watch over us. She told us that we needed to watch T.V. together, plus do other things together, so that we would bond.

"Peggy, I am happy to tell you that your mother and I have had this bond from the day we were wed. Along life's road, we have added to this bond by attaching glue, solder, chains, fetters, shackles, and even handcuffs, and at our 50th wedding anniversary or shortly after, we had the local blacksmith weld us together. We have now dropped our personal identity because we are as one——so Peggy, set your mind at ease. Your mother and I are bonded."

When the feminist movement first started, it scared the living tar out of me. I am sure that the people who had the initiative behind this movement liked women better than men, but even when they first started, I could see some good in this. If women wanted to fall off the pedestal that men had placed them on, so be it. Equal opportunity and equal pay is the American way of life, and I am for it, especially now that I have five grandbabies that are either already in the workforce or are soon to enter. May the force be with them.

My problem is with the females, who think that they have to be in the combat arms of our military or in police or fire units. Women are the weaker sex physically. Don't you think that God knew that when He made us, and don't you think He knew that we would worship someone soft and curvy? Of course, the "pump iron babes" would tell you that I am full of you know what. In my military days, it would have killed my body and soul to see a female put into a body bag. Even now it would be distasteful to be a party to this action. What I think I am trying to say is go as far as you want to go, but please stay a woman. Maintain the nesting quality and motherhood, and the males will love you forever.

I have no magic formula for a long and happy marriage except for two people to truly love each other. That love will have to be deep enough to be able to overlook their partner's faults, which every human being possesses. I do not want to turn into a male Ann Landers. I just want to pass on to my granddaughters and great-grands some thoughts that this old country boy has accumulated in over fifty years of marriage. I had the privilege of meeting Ann Landers at the L.B.J. Ranch when she was visiting there, and I flew her home to Chicago. I want to go on the record and tell you that I did not ask her for any advice on love and marriage. Therefore, all this crap you have been reading comes from yours truly.

The one thing that I have observed, which has been brought into the daylight from the feminist movement, is the monetary aspect of marriage. Now we have her money, his money, and our money. This has probably helped to destroy more marriages than infidelity. This is a really tough issue that has to be solved by the two partners as they go down the road of life. It is not easy, but it can be worked out. In most cases, the "give and take" aspect of marriage will prevail. One will give in, and the other one will have the financial responsibility for the family cell.

I have a few do's and do not's, and please take them with a grain of salt. You and I and everyone else in the world have heard the advice given to all married couples, "Never go to sleep while you are still mad at each other."

There are several options available to partners. Do not talk to your mate while in the love nest, but concentrate on how you will be able to get even with her. Once you have figured this out, you will sleep like a baby. Or you can talk things out with an apology of regrets from all parties. Then have a kiss and make-up time. I prefer the latter because that is so much more fun than the new day bringing the storm clouds down upon you. Or you could do nothing. Just let this little dispute fester and fester until it eats up the guts of both parties. Then take it to a divorce court where you end up sawing the children in half.

Each partner needs independence without limitations, unless it adversely affects others in the family cell. We have always been able to talk things out, and we come to a solution for the good of all. This has to be one of the answers to our longevity in marriage.

Private time or what we call "alone time" is very important also. Health is the only factor that would interrupt the alone time. If one mate is ill, then of course, the other would be in attendance. This works for us. I am happy to be able to get in my pickup truck and go to the ranch to feed and care for our cows. We are into this wireless thing, so we can stay in touch with each other. Just to be alone with only your thoughts for company for a few hours a day is wonderful, and this makes me happy. I have a sneaking suspicion that it makes Libby even happier.

"If I had done this or if I had done that" is a part of everyone's life. The good Lord guides us all in different ways that are in compliance with his overall plan. So when he steered us to President Johnson and his family, it was carved into solid rock. We were to be influenced by this family until the end of our time. When we count our blessings, and we have so many, it should include this family, who has meant so much to us.

We have faith; we have family; we have friends, and we have had a lot of fun traveling down life's road. I have all this, plus I have an ace in the hole. I have Libby, and we will be together for all eternity.

GLOSSARY

AAF Army Air Force (became a separate branch of service called United States Air Force in 1948).

ADF Automatic Directional Finder (a device for finding out the direction from which radio waves or signals are coming).

AFB Air Force Base.

AMPI American Milk Producers Inc.

APC Armed Personnel Carrier (light armor––troop carrier with mounted machine gun).

ARVN Army of Republic of Vietnam (South Vietnamese soldiers).

Bangalore Linear explosives, used by both sides in combat.

Bivouac Temporary encampment (especially of soldiers in the open with only tents or improvised shelter).

C.I.A. Central Intelligence Agency.

Clinker A hard mass of fused stony matter formed in a firebox from impurities in the coal.

C.O. Commanding Officer.

Crypto Equipment used in being such secretly, not by public avowal.

Dinks The enemy. This term became dominant in the later years of the war in Vietnam.

F.A.A. Federal Aviation Agency.

Fastmovers Jet Aircraft.

F-4 Phantom-fighter-bomber, manufactured by McDonnell.

Fjords A narrow inlet or arm of the sea bordered by steep cliffs, especially in Norway.

G.E. Turbines Jet power plant built by General Electric.

Guard Emergency Radio Frequency.

Head Boat Charge each person by the head to take you deep sea fishing.

IFR Instrument Flight Regulations (does not mean, I Follow Railroads).

I Corps The most northern of four geographical divisions of South Vietnam, designated for military convenience.

KP Duty Kitchen Police Duty.

M.P. Military Police.

LCT Landing Craft Transport.

NVA North Vietnamese Army.

N601T FAA number on our King Air Aircraft––there for our call sign.

P.O.E. Port of Embarkation.

P.O.W. Prisoner of War.

P.S.P. Perforated steel plate––sectional, interlocking steel panels used to produce a hard surface for runways or flight lines.

RHIP Rank Has Its Privileges.

RIF Reduction in Force.

R.O.T.C. Reserve Officer Training Corps.

R & R Rest and Recreation.

RPM Revolutions per minute.

SAM Surface-to-air missile.

SIP Standardization Instructor Pilot.

Shitcan Half a 55-gallon drum used in latrines, burned with diesel fuel when needed.

S.S. Secret Service Agent.

Teutonic North European group of people, including German, Scandinavian, Dutch, English, etc.

TNT Trinitrotoluene (explosive).

Translational Lift An aerodynamic lifting force applied to helicopters by obtaining an airspeed of 12 to 15 knots.

U-2 Aircraft capable of high altitude and endurance.

USO United Service Organizations.

V.C. Viet Cong.

Printed in the United States
By Bookmasters